PLAN OF

...TON MANOR ESTATE

...LBANS, HERTFORDSHIRE.

For Sale by

MESS.RS STIMPSON. LOCK & VINCE,

(WATFORD, BUSHEY, NORTHWOOD & PINNER,)

JUNE 6TH

1923.

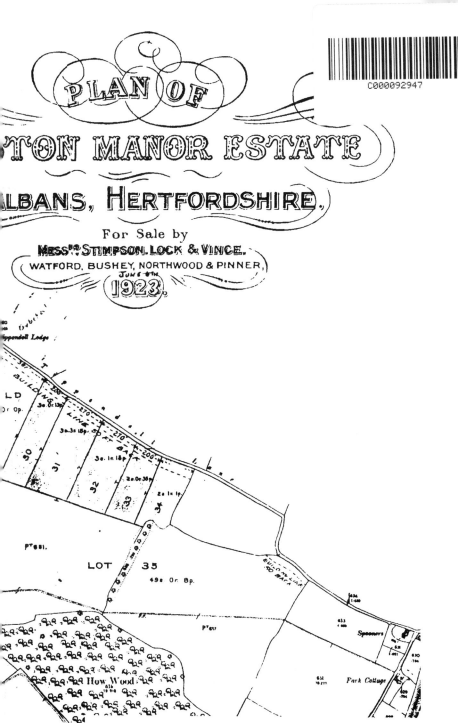

ppendell Lodge

LD
Or Op.

3a. 0r. 13p

3a.3r. 15p.

30

31

3a. 1n. 18p.

32

2a.0r.35p

33

2a.1r.1p

34

PT 31.

LOT 35

49a 0r. 8p.

BUILDING LINE 50 FT BACK

How Wood

PT 17

Spooners

Park Cottage

Park Street's Past

Cyril H. Martin

Verulam Publishing

Dedication

I dedicate this book to all those members, present and in the future, of the Park Street & Frogmore Preservation Society, of which I am proud to be President. Hoping that they will grow in status and strength and become an everlasting bulwark against any harmful influences that may affect our small district now, and for many years to come.

Acknowledgements

I wish to give my very warm thanks to the whole range of people, near and far, who have supported the making of this history. A very special thanks to Geoffrey and Jean Taylor, the last private owners of Moormill, who supplied without question sixteen important documents about the early life to their mill. Also Peggy Braybrook and Eileen Smith who very willingly gave access to all their father's records on the Park Valley Estate. To Margaret Young for the family bible records found in Australia. To the Chapman brothers for photographs and details about the last days of the Park Street mill. To Roger Shepherd for the help and support he has freely given me in my research. To the Bricketwood Society for some details on the Moormill owners list. To the Thistle Hotel Group plc for sending me documents concerning their Noke Hotel. To Ian Honeywood for some photographic work. Not forgetting a heartfelt thanks to those newspapers, Herts Advertiser, Herald, St Albans and Watford Observer and The Review .. that have given me considerable backing throughout the writing of my three local histories.

The publisher wishes to acknowledge the considerable editorial help and advise given by Harry and Joan Collins and to Joan for typing the manuscript.

Published in Great Britain 1995 by Verulam Publishing Ltd.,
152a Park Street Lane, Park Street, St Albans, Hertfordshire AL2 2AU

ISBN: 1 874504 09 1

Printed in Great Britain by BPC Wheatons Ltd, Exeter

Contents

	Acknowledgements	page	ii
	Introduction	page	iv
Chapter 1	The Hamlet of Parkye and the Status of Blacksmiths on Saxon Times	page	1
Chapter 2	Village Life Under the Normans	page	3
Chapter 3	The Village in Secular Hands	page	11
Chapter 4	The Ancient Property of Moor Mill - Past & Present	page	22
Chapter 5	Memories of a Lively Moor Mill	page	38
Chapter 6	Smiths & Workers in Iron	page	43
Chapter 7	Return to Park Street	page	48
Chapter 8	Some Interesting Features of Ancient Radlett and its Early Proprietors	page	57
Chapter 9	Documents Concerning the Wigg Family Mentioning Property in Park Valley Estate	page	69
Chapter 10	History of Burston Manor	page	80
Chapter 11	Lye House	page	90
Chapter 12	The Settled Land Acts 1882 - 1890	page	98
	Index	page	107

Foreword

As the director of a visionary environmental initiative which will bring about significant landscape changes to a wide area including Park Street, I am delighted that Cyril Martin has written another notable book which chronicles the history of this area.

It is so important to understand and respect the past uses and ownership patterns of our local landscape and to use the expertise of these landowners and farmers who worked in tune with the natural elements, to help guide future land use management. Local historical research brings fascinating insights into our familiar local surrounding and I am sure that this third book of Cyril Martin's will be of great interest to many people living in and around Park Street.

Catherine Cairns
Watling Chase Project Director.

INTRODUCTION
PARK STREET'S PAST
THE MILLERS, BLACKSMITHS AND PROPRIETORS OF OLD PARK STREET

The census of 1891 which comprised 560 pages and was not published until August 1893 showed that the County of Hertfordshire population had grown by a figure of 12,804. Millers and blacksmiths formed but a small section of the 711 occupations enumerated. The returns were divided into six main classes. The industrial class of that period showed an extraordinary increase in the number of females taking up black-smithing, bricklaying, carpentering, painting and even chimney-sweeping, as if to prove that the emancipation of women had come about long before the suffragette movement of the early 20th century.

Hertfordshire has fostered many a cottage industry in the past - straw-plaiting, seed-sorting, book-binding and basket making. These grew up in the villages, even in tiny hamlets, before moving into the towns; but wherever there was a river, brook or stream, milling and blacksmithing seemed to have been the principal, if not the only, form of industry.

Most people are well aware how the streams are used to drive a mill, but how many know the vital importance of water to a black-smith? They may have watched him quench his hot iron in the big tank always present at the forge, but probably knew little of its other uses. Smithy-coal is a small grained, high-combustion fuel, and must be mixed with water to a plastic consistency that enables the smith to build a furnace around awkward shaped pieces of iron. The heat can then go to the right place and maintain the shape of the fire against the strong blast from the bellows - a process which consumes almost as much water as coal. Bearing in mind these facts, one would think that wherever there was a mill, a blacksmith's shop would not be far away.

CHAPTER 1

THE HAMLET OF PARKYE AND THE STATUS OF

BLACKSMITHS IN SAXON TIMES

Before the Saxon invasion only a few houses existed here in what is now the village of Park Street. They were built in Roman style. It was a convenient 'stopping place' in those days, for a rest from a tedious journey, a meal in comfort or a repair to whatever transport had been used. Its first inhabitants were probably Romano-British but there is no doubt that they very soon adopted the 'Saxon way of life'.

Saxon men spent most of their time practising the art of war with spear and shield. They toughened their bodies by performing feats of strength and endurance. Although they gathered together in war or council they preferred to live apart, each with his own family. No houses were built adjacent to each other; each family had its own strip of land which was cultivated by the women. Oxen were used for ploughing. The men cleared a part of the forest to make pasture for their beasts. The crops they grew were chiefly grain with a long straw, used for thatching. Each household ground its own flour with a family 'quern'; but their diet consisted largely of milk, cheese and flesh. Only the overlords had their grain ground by a water-mill. The overlords were deemed to be Ceorls or Theodens, that is men who had gained prowess in battle or leadership.

A Ceorl or Theoden occupied the most important house on each estate. That house became known, after the Conquest, as a manor house. The one belonging to the estate of Parkye was situated east of the railway line at Colney Street on a site now occupied by a farmhouse near a gravel works. The one at Burston still stands near the Orbital by-pass almost alongside the Burston-Tyler garden shop. No manor house was ever built for the inhospitable Estate of Eywood. The Saxons developed only the northern part of it, near the monastery. The rest con-

1

sisted of dense woods, undergrowth and thickets, through which the water, spreading out over the flat valley, wound a tortuous path among masses of brush, thorns and coarse grasses, leaving behind shallow pools, bogs and swamps where there was "no path for man or beast" as one Saxon chronicler aptly said.

Although there were no millers here in Saxon times, there were plenty of blacksmiths who made weapons, armorial clothing (chain corselets) and a wide range of agricultural and household articles, all made of iron. Despite his importance and his skill, the blacksmith had no status in the Saxon community. His job fell into the category of all those men of his time who had no battle experience. They, together with the older men, were treated almost as slaves. Records show that households belonging to Saxon men of fighting rank were often swollen by a number of these workers, skilled and unskilled, who lived with them and did most of the work.

An Early English record book, namely the Codex Diplomaticus quotes a will made by a Saxon lady to free all the slaves of her household. The following is an extract from that will:

Geatflaed freed for God's sake and for her soul's need, namely, Ecceard, the smith and Aelfstan and his wife and all their offspring born and unborn; and Arcil and Cole and Ecgferth, Aadhun's daughter, and all the men who bent their heads for food in the evil days.

In the years that followed, most blacksmiths who had been attached to a particular Saxon household obtained their freedom but it was not until after the Norman Conquest that their trade became the treasured and important one it so well deserved to be.

CHAPTER 2

VILLAGE LIFE UNDER THE NORMANS

Immediately after the Norman Conquest, William sent emissaries all over the country to assess the wealth of his new kingdom. It was twenty years before their work came to be compiled into the famous Domesday Book, which accounted for all lands and properties and the income derived from them at the end of the Saxon period.

The first Norman abbot, Paul de Caen, took over all the terrain once controlled by the Saxon abbot at St. Albans Monastery. One of his first tasks was to pull down most of the Saxon monastic buildings that had been inhabited by 'nuns' as well as monks since 793 AD. Remains of the old Saxon buildings lie somewhere beneath the foundations of the Abbey.

In the years that followed a new monastery was constructed and members of the same order were installed; monks only this time.

During the long years it took to construct the new monastery the abbot and his staff introduced new taxes, fees and dues and imposed fines for misdemeanours. A weekly Court was held to deal with the affairs of the district. It replaced the Saxon monthly Wapentake or Hundred Court. The punishment meted out by the Norman Court was recorded in a Court Roll. Only one, dated October 23rd, 1348, has survived. Several Parke Court books which carried extracts from these rolls have been preserved in the British Library. One book stated that there were seventy-seven monks and about a hundred servants and tradesmen living, at that particular time, within the confines of the monastery.

The Norman 'mark' had followed William over the Channel and many dues and assessments were quoted in the Norman currency. The mark was valued at thirteen Anglo-Saxon shillings and four pence -

probably due to the odd four pence involved, a silver fourpenny piece came to be minted.

During the years 1146 to 1167 the monastery funds were getting low. The abbot at that time, probably Geoffrey de Gorham or his nephew Robert, decided to build more mills and charge a fee for the grinding of corn. The three mills near the monastery were busy at that time in 'fulling' the people's cloth, obviously at a considerable profit to the abbot. Suitable places along the rivers controlled by the monastery were surveyed. The diffused waters in the Eywood estate were considered unsuitable to power a mill. It was found necessary to divert the river near Sopwell and make it follow a course hugging the North West foothills. To prevent the new stream from flowing back over the flat valley it was banked up with timber cut from the Eywood forest mixed with clay and chalk. A generous proportion of the people around Eywood and Parke at that time were serfs and slaves, so one can guess who did most of the work involved.

When the job had been done to the abbot's satisfaction, a head of water was obtained at the hamlet sufficient to operate an over-shot water-wheel. The first mill was constructed from trees felled on the spot and hewed into shape with the rough tools of that period. It could only have been two storeys high with a thatched roof and was built near one of the houses in the hamlet that the Saxon Abbot Leofstan (the 12th or last but one Saxon abbot) had requisitioned or built in 1045 to shelter pilgrims *en route* to the Shrine of St. Alban.

After working the mill the water was returned to the old river bed. The by-pass stream also returned there, through a sluice gate and a waterfall.

Once the mill was in working order the people of the district were compelled to bring their corn there to be ground into flour, being charged a fee, in coin or in kind. Even before that time many of their daily activities were restricted. They had to pay a fine called *chevage* if

4

they left the manor; they weren't allowed to trespass on the abbot's fields or woods. Trees were not to be cut down without permission; poaching in the woods was a punishable offence. Fines were extracted for the neglect of their 'holdings', which could not be transferred without the consent of the reeve. In theory, all the lower class women of the district were considered as chattels of the abbot. They had to obtain his permission to marry and even if that was granted, a due known as *merchet* had to be paid. Sometimes, if a woman had previously lived with a man or had a child out of wedlock, she was compelled to pay an additional fine called *leyrwite*.

Anyone caught fishing in the abbot's waters (all rivers, ponds and lakes of the district) suffered a severe penalty.

During the years following the building of the mill, the population of the hamlet continued to increase. At the time of Richard de Wallingford, the 15th Norman abbot, the mill lands were extended, the river widened and deepened and several outbuildings constructed, one of them being a workshop where repairs to the mill machinery could be done more efficiently.

Richard was the orphaned son of a blacksmith, a man whose intellect and mechanical knowledge was far ahead of his time. He had no immediate relations after his parents died and was adopted by William Kirkby, a prior of the order of Benedictines who sent him to Oxford to study, judging him to have remarkable intelligence for one so young. There are extensive records of his mathematical ability, skill and achievements in the Bodleian Library at Oxford. On leaving Oxford he came to St. Albans monastery as an ordinary monk. Within a short time his obvious superior intellect caused him to be elected abbot.

Shortly after becoming abbot, he and several of his staff visited France, a slow process in those days, to pay homage to the Pope at Avignon. On that journey he could have noticed a French smith engaged in making cast-iron parts for mills or other pieces of machinery and learned of its good wearing properties. The small forge and foundry that was used in the Parkye mill workshop during his term of office was, without doubt, set up under his personal direction, because the pipes that fed the strong stream of air from the continuous-blast bellows to the furnace were marked in French. Similar bellows and equipment were found in the workshop attached to the mill at Park Street. My family took over this workshop at the latter end of the 17th century and two of its draught pipes were marked in French. Richard de Wallingford had installed the workshop there about the year 1330 and it was almost in ruins when my family took it over.

Quite recently, sketches of a clock that Richard had designed were found in the Bodleian Library at Oxford. A clock has been made from them and installed in St. Albans Abbey. One has only to look at its construction to realise that there was something of the 'blacksmith' still lurking in his highly educated mind. He knew enough about isochronism to regulate the escapement of his clock with a dual weighted horizontal balance, hundreds of years before Galileo invented the pendulum or Newton had thought up the Laws of Motion. Richard's balance became a guide to the making of the chronometer 'balance' of the early 19th century, which enabled us to make precise maps of any place on the Earth's surface.

Richard wrote this prayer to God not long before his death on 23rd May, 1336.

I recall to myself how, although I was of lowly birth
Thou did'st raise me from the dung and did'st lead me
forth from the cottage of my father and did'st so honour
me that I sit among princes and occupy a glorious
throne. So whereof shall I be silent?
Thou gavest me the task of pasturing the flock of Thy
people and wentest with me in all my goings.
(Richard's prayer is translated from the *Gesta Abbaticum*

held in the British Library in London.)

How fortunate that he spared a little of his genius to improve the working of the mill in our own small locality.

In 1400 John Moote, the 18th Norman abbot, rebuilt the Parkyemyll and leased it for an indeterminate period to John Wyndsor, a yeoman of Sergehill.

By 1527 it had passed into the possession of John Redwood, who held it on a thirty-one year lease, copyhold to the Manor of Parke. He paid an annual rent of six pounds. One of the conditions of his lease, which was signed by William Abraham as representing the Lord of the Manor, was that he, John Redwood, must keep the mill and all the 'millterre' in good repair, using timber cut from the woods at Byrchthead (Bricket Wood). During that period came evidence of the names of two Park Street blacksmiths.

Extract of Will (From *Herts Genealogist and Antiquary*)

> 'Johannes Benne of Parkstret (*die lune post festum Inventionis sancte*) date 1407, buried at St. Stephens. Henry Cony, clerk, William Cony, clerk, wife Matilda and Margery daughter of William Ffraunceys, blacksmith of Parkstret, executors. Nicholas Clerke and said William Ffraunceys, supervisors.'

Trading License (From *Gibbs Corporation Records*)

> 'John Ffrancys of Park Street, blacksmith, was secured to sell wine on market days and fair days within the Borough on a quarterly payment of 4d to the Wardens of each company (dated 3rd January, 1586).'

1539 saw the end of a period lasting 740 years under the rule of the monastery of St. Albans. During the latter part the Hamlet of Parkye became the Village of Park Street.

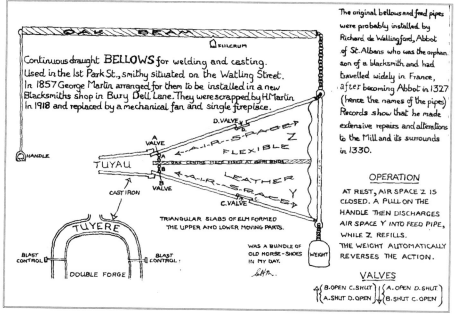

The original bellows and feed pipes were probably installed by Richard de Wallingford, Abbot of St.Albans who was the orphan son of a blacksmith and had travelled widely in France, after becoming Abbot in 1327 (hence the names of the pipes) Records show that he made extensive repairs and alterations to the Mill and its surrounds in 1330.

OPERATION

AT REST, AIR SPACE Z IS CLOSED. A PULL ON THE HANDLE THEN DISCHARGES AIR SPACE Y INTO FEED PIPE, WHILE Z REFILLS. THE WEIGHT AUTOMATICALLY REVERSES THE ACTION.

VALVES

(B.OPEN C.SHUT) (A. OPEN D.SHUT)
(A.SHUT D. OPEN) (B. SHUT C. OPEN)

Continuous draught BELLOWS for welding and casting. Used in the 1st Park St., smithy situated on the Watling Street. In 1857 George Martin arranged for them to be installed in a new Blacksmiths shop in Bury Dell Lane. They were scrapped by H.Martin In 1918 and replaced by a mechanical fan and single fireplace.

Sketch of the ancient bellows used for casting and smithing in Park Street.

Abbey premiere

ST Albans Chamber Choir is giving the first performance of a new work by award-winning young British composer Alan Stones in the Abbey on Saturday.

Entitled Verses and Carillons, the work is scored for chamber choir, percussion and live electronics and has been composed with the particular architecture of St Albans Abbey in mind.

The libretto draws on material from the Abbey archives and the work is based on the writings and work of Richard of Wallingford who was Abbot of St Albans Abbey in the 14th century.

The concert will be conducted by Richard Stangroom and starts at 7.30pm. Other works on the programme include Mozart's Vesperae solennes de confessore, Allegri's Miserere and Lotti's Crucifixus.

Article in *The Herts Advertiser* 9 June 1993 (Reproduced by kind permission)

Time marches on at Abbey

AN 11-year project to recreate a 14th century astronomical clock which once stood in St Alban Abbey is nearing completion.

And the team of men who have worked on the scheme will start to assemble their latest section later this week as their farewell to the Dean of St Albans, the Very Rev Peter Moore, who is retiring.

Project co-ordinator John Attewill said: "It was the Dean's idea that the clock should be recreated and we wanted to show him how far we have got before he retires next month."

The original clock was completed at the Abbey in 1336 under Abbot Richard of Wallingford who spent a great deal of time designing it.

The clock showed at all times the position of the sun, moon, stars and lunar eclipses.

The original clock disappeared at around the time of the dissolution of the monastery and it was not until this century that Abbot Richard's rough notes giving mathematics, gear ratios and some sketches were found in the Bodleian

By JOHN MANNING

Library, Oxford.

But the St Albans team has had to do much of its own design work and, latterly a team of only four or five people have been working on the clock.

The first phase, the horologe, which makes one revolution in 24 hours, was completed five years ago and has been in the Abbey's North Transept since then.

The last remaining pie ＾ of the clock to be completed will be the section which shows the eclipses.

Mr Attewill said: "The whole thing will be completed and running by Christmas."

Article from the *Herts Advertiser* of 28 September 1993
(Reproduced by kind permission)

Time for old time at Abbey

A TIME-KEEPING relic from St Albans' past has reappeared at the city's cathedral.

Although it is not the original, the copy of the old Wallingford Clock has been carefully constructed and made by its creator, Abbot Richard of Wallingford. ib. (2/2)

Richard was elected Abbot of St Albans monastery in 1327, but died in 1336 before the clock was completed.

In their spare time a group of enthusiasts from the Abbey congregation and from the St Albans Engineering Society, have been making a full scale model of the clock.

Work will continue over winter until the model is in full working order, driven by weights.

The original not only told the time but showed the positions of the sun, moon and planets as well as lunar eclipses.

It disappeared around the time of the dissolution of the monastery, but this century rough notes of its construction were found in the Bodlean Library, Oxford.

Two engineering replicas have already been made and one is in a horological museum in the United States.

The Wallingford Clock is seen here taking pride of place in the North Transept of the Cathedral.

Article from the *St Albans Observer* of 23 November 1988
(Reproduced by kind permission)

CHAPTER 3

THE VILLAGE IN SECULAR HANDS

After the Dissolution, Henry the Eighth gave the Monastery of St. Albans together with the northern part of Eywood Estate, to Sir Richard Lee, a military engineer who had gained favour by his prowess in warfare. He sold the monastery and adjacent land for 890 marks to Richard Boreman the last of the abbots, who had retired quite a wealthy man, having done some clever dealing in church property just before the takeover. The abbots always dealt in 'marks' whenever possible.

That part of Eywood Estate which included Park Street, Lee gave to his son-in-law Humphrey Conningsby. In 1600 it became the property of another Richard - Richard Francklyn, a gentleman.

It wasn't until 1731 that a record came giving the actual size of the mill property. At that time it was owned by Thomas Babbs. The accounts gave the mill lands to consist of 7 acres, 3 roods and 16 poles. The property eventually passed from Babbs to a man named Samuel J. Dagnall. He was an elder of the Parish of St. Peter, St. Albans. His will, dated 1762, is in the archives at Hertford. It mentions the corn mill, gardens, barns, outbuildings with appurtenances and commodities, watercourses, a meadow called Pickbourne, a cart shed and the mill house occupied by his son John. At that particular date only the three-storey section of the house attached to the mill had been built.

The cart shed mentioned in the will was subsequently rented by the Hertfordshire Union to hold chapel services. Although the village had been under religious rule for nearly seven and a half centuries, that cart shed was the first place of worship located in the village.

During the time that the mill was owned by Thomas Babbs, a journeyman named Larkin was working there as a miller. He was married to a local woman named Jane Veary. A son was born to them

11

on the twenty-first day of November 1732. They named him John. Two years afterwards, the Larkins moved to Frogmore mill at Hempsted, where Jane died in 1736 giving birth to another child. The baby also died. Both are buried in Hempsted churchyard.

John and his father spent the rest of their lives working in mills in Hertfordshire and Buckinghamshire. At the age of eleven his father put John to a Free school in Amersham. From then on John kept a diary about history, family life, mills and rivers. He dedicated it to God and called it his Atom. That diary brought him fame as an historian, perhaps uniquely so, for one so lowly born. His Atom gives a delightful account of life on the rivers and mills as he travelled around them during those early years.

Also about that time there are records of two Park Street blacksmiths, Tom Alding in 1727 and Will Shepherd in 1736.

Thomas Goddard held the mill property from 1802-1839. He was one of those proprietors, of which there were many, who could enjoy a full life on the proceeds from the land he owned, which enabled him to take part in a great many of the social activities of the county. Being a member of the Hertfordshire Hunt he frequently 'rode to hounds' with some of the elite in the county. In his time the Master of the Hunt was Mr Delme Radcliffe of Hitchen Priory, who also kept a diary. One particular 'chase' that Thomas took part in was recorded as being the most 'extraordinary run' in the annals of Hertfordshire. One horse died from exhaustion, others became too tired to finish. The whole chase covered twenty-six miles in two hours, twenty-five minutes, and still the wily fox eluded them. Thomas was accompanied on that day by the huntsman William Boxall, Jem Simpkins a whipper-in, mounted on his famous horse 'Pippin', the Hon. E. Grimston from Gorhambury, and Messrs. E.T. Daniel, M. Evans and Mr Hayward of St. Albans.

It was probably Thomas Goddard who made the arrangement

for the hunt to meet under the giant horse-chestnut tree at Spooner's Corner. One obvious reason why the hunt came there quite often was because the stables behind the tree were fitted out with special lavatories for 'Ladies that rode to hounds'.

George and Ann Beament took over the mill from Thomas Goddard. They came to Park Street from New Barnes. The Beaments were farmers by tradition as well as millers. George and Ann had eight children, two girls and six boys. The eldest, Edwin, was born in 1831. Then a daughter followed in 1840. After them came George Joseph 1842, Will Henry 1844, Charles 1846, James Alfred 1849, another daughter in 1852, followed by their youngest son James Marcus in 1854.

The Beaments hadn't been in the village long before they set about rebuilding the last of the timber mills in attractive red and grey brick, in a style common during the Industrial Revolution. They did away with most of the old timber structures that surrounded the mill, including the ancient workshop, but kept the chimney-stack and turned that part into a bakehouse; at the same time they reinforced some of the old flint walls along the river and around the garden with brickwork. At that period there was no brick bridge over the by-pass stream in Burydell Lane which ran further along, parallel to the lane, and joined the bed of the ancient river near where there had once been a ford. The present bridge was built in 1866, but before that another smithy work-shop was built in the mid 19th century to replace the one bordering the main street, which was demolished. The new smithy backed on to the terminating high wall of the mill kitchen garden; indeed, that wall formed one side of the smithy and the blacksmith was asked to pay a nominal rent for it. It was a gentleman's agreement between George Beament and George Martin and the building never appeared on the mill plans until 1906.

Following the Beament's arrival two members of the Warren

family worked as millers there - George Warren in 1840 and Tom Warren in 1846. The new brick mill was finished in 1846. In 1852 George Beament acquired the White Horse farm and was managing both. In 1860 he was running the Park Valley farm while his son William Henry had the mill jointly with his brother James Alfred in 1873. Unfortunately, James suffered from a serious illness and died in Arlesley Asylum when he was only 33.

By 1888 Edwin, known to his contemporaries as Teddy, had the mill, while Marcus, known as Marky, was farming at Park Valley. Their youngest sister had married William Chaffy Giddins, commonly known as Chaffy, a wealthy yeoman farmer living at Mimms Hall. He had been paying rent for some years to the Wigg family at Frogmore house for the use of one of the fields in Burydell. After the death of her parents his wife persuaded him to make her brothers an offer for the mill. Edwin and Marcus agreed, and a down payment was made in 1895. At the same time they contracted to collect the rent for the blacksmith's shop for him and also for the two cottages to the rear of the mill front yard, occupied at that time by Bluffy Barnes and George Gurney.

Chaffy died on the first of May 1905. His will provided that a sum of one thousand pounds be paid to the Beament brothers (obviously to complete the mill deal). The executors of the will then put up the property to be sold by auction in 1906. Chaffy's third son Stanley Giddins then bought the property and he and his wife came to live at Park Street in the mill house. Edwin and Marcus had moved out and taken two cottages fronting the main street where Edwin started a milk shop and general store. Stanley and his wife Helen had four boys: Cliff, Eustace, Dudley and Leslie, and one girl, Nancy. Another girl, Joan Helen Mary, died in infancy. The mill was prosperous in those days. Corn from the local farms was ground into flour then transported to the London markets. Stabling and storage space was ample. The triangular field between the mill by-pass and the main stream became a free-range chicken farm, watched over by Jack Garratt. He was also the mill wagon driver and stableman. The miller, George Wheeler, lived in the cottage now known as Toll Cottage. He had a busy time working the mill every day except Sunday. Often there were queues of carts waiting in the mill front yard and Burydell Lane for a turn to go under the projecting sack-lifts. Farmers, dealers and many of his gambling friends pulled up their horses and traps to park outside the office in the main street. There were no parking laws in those days - no pavements either, everybody walked in the middle of the road.

The mill office was situated on the second floor of the older part of the house at the Dell corner. One had to negotiate a flight of three stone steps to get to the door. Beneath the office was a cellar where wine and spirits were stored. It served as a shelter from Zeppelin raids during the Great War. Not only did Stanley do business there but he spent a lot of time gambling there with his friends. He also converted one of the old outbuildings in the mill front garden for entertainment purposes. It contained a billiard table but was also used for parties and meetings.

Brimley Villas had already been built on the garden further north. They were built on the site of an old timber-built house used for storing and repairing the boats used in keeping the mill water courses free. Each year, at the end of the summer season, these boats were borrowed by the Park Street Minstrels who would decorate them, supply a crew of musicians and organise a tuneful, colourful water regatta that would voyage slowly upstream accompanied by many other boats from the houses that backed on to the river.

Helen Giddins played hostess to dancing classes held in the new part of the house for some of the village children. Her own children were quite accomplished. They organised concerts and plays which took place in one of the barns backing on to the kitchen garden.

15

PROGRAMME

(The Old School, Branch Road)

❋ PART I ❋

1. Piano Duet   "Qui Vive"   *Ganz*
     Mrs Doris Roskilly & Miss Gladys Isles
2. Song   "When Shadows Gather" *Marshall*
     Miss Bailey
3. Banjo Duet   "Cromartie"   *Heath*
     Clifton Giddins & Tom Handscomb
4. Skirt Dance
5. Cornet Solo   "The Lost Chord"   *Sullivan*
     Mr Slade
Clarke
6. Vocal Duet   Life's Dream is o'er   *Ascher*
7. Duologue   Editha's Burglar   *Burnett*
     Editha   Miss Doris Elderd
     The Burglar   Mr. Gerald Eldred
8. Song   "A Song of Surrey"   *Hermann Lohr*
     Mr. C. Howard
9. Scotch Reel
     Doris & Daisy Grey, Nancy Giddins & Doris Martin.
10. Violin Solo   Selected
     Mr. Alan Gladwell
11. Recitation   "A Pastoral Play"   *Mel. B. Spurr*
     Miss. Bamforth
12. Song   "Three Green Bonnets"   *Guy d'Hardelot*
     Mrs. O. Wood.
13. Dance   "A Society Dance"
     Miss Doris Eldred
14. Banjo Solo
     Mr. Will Howard
15. Comic Song   Selected

❋ PART II ❋

16. Piano Duet   "March Around the Maypole"
     Olive Costin & Clifton Giddins
17. Song   "Sincerity"   *Emily Clark*
     Miss Bailey
18. Sash Dance
     Hilda & Kitty Wright, Olive Costin & Ada Tansley
19. Cornet Solo "Oh Dry Those Tears" *Teresa del Riego*
20. Sailors' Hornpipe
     Clifton, Dudley, Eustace Giddins, Fred Isles & Leonard
21. Piano Solo   Faryland Waltz   *C Warren*
22. Recitation   Selected
     Miss Bamforth
23. Vocal Duet   "Venetian Song"   *Tosti*
     Miss O. Wright & Mrs. O. Wood
24. Banjo Solo   Mr. Will Howard
25. Song   "Marie my Girl"   *G. Aitkin*
     Mr. C. Howard
26. Dance   "The Sunbonnet Lady"
     Miss Doris Elderd
27. Trio   "Sweet & Low"   *Barnaby*
     Miss O. Wright, Mrs. O. Wood, Mr. F. Wright.
28. Violin Solo   Selected
     Mr. Alan Gladwell
29. Song   "Across the Blue Sea"   *Lord Henry Somerset*
     Miss O. Wood
30. Comic Song   Selected
     Mr. Harold Pusey
Accompanist ... ... Mrs. STANLEY GIDDINS

"GOD SAVE THE KING"

Above: Reproduction of the programme of a village concert held in the Old School, Branch Road in 1912 These prosperous years continued for the Giddins family until the end of the first World War, when Stanley became mentally ill and had to be taken away to hospital. He was heavily in debt and the property had to be put up for sale. It was bought by Ronald Beach Christmas, a chicken farmer from Abbotts Langley.

The last of the flour mills

Shortly after Stanley Giddins died his family left the district. After the sale of the mill property Helen, his wife, came back once or twice to visit her son Cliff who had taken a house in Tippingdell Lane some

16

years after his father died. He lived there for a while with his daughter April before moving to Southend. They were the only ones of the Giddins family to witness the decline of the majestic old flour mill into a monstrous glue factory, after serving the district for almost 750 years, grinding its corn and making employment for the inhabitants.

Ronald Christmas came to the village with big ideas. The days of corn-grinding were over for his mill, the Co-op had obtained a monopoly in this area. It was he who turned the mill into a glue factory. The water-wheels were disconnected, much of the belt-driven shafting removed, the grind-stones taken out and left in the mill back yard awaiting sale. Most of the corn storage space was taken up by a series of galvanised troughs. The chain sack-lifts were replaced by a steam driven lift taking a van-load of bones. A part of the wall facing Burydell Lane was knocked out to give access. A new boiler house was built in the mill backyard to make steam to power the machinery and 'digest' the bones. A huge metal column serving as a 'digester' stood erect through three floors. It was fed at the top with the bones from the lift. During the operation liquid glue passed from the digester into a network of pipes feeding a series of galvanised cooling troughs.

That process and the obnoxious smell it created went on for nearly four years. The villagers began to wish that they had never had a 'Christmas'. Their suffering came to an end about 1924 when he sold the mill and moved to Bricket Wood to start a funfair called Joyland, in opposition to a fair ground called Woodside Retreat that had been operating there since 1889.

The mill property was bought by Captain Harry Hopkinson and his wife Cordelia. After his career in the Army, Harry seemed to have no interest in the mill, either as a building or as a business. It stood for years just as Christmas had left it, smelly and becoming over-run with rats.

The Hopkinsons were an impressive couple, both over six feet tall. Harry claimed to have met his wife in France when she was Cordelia Granville, a nurse at the hospital where he was recovering from a bayonet wound in the leg. His wounded leg caused him to walk in a manner that soon earned him the nickname of Hoppy. With his army tales and his abortive attempts to sell what was left of the glue in the mill, he became a well-known figure in the village, especially in the pubs where he regaled the customers with his army experiences.

Because of its proximity to an aerodrome this district suffered some heavy bombing during the Second World War. Hoppy told several people that bombs had dislodged one of the mill's water-wheels.

During the war he leased the mill, first to a firm known as Zinnemans as a store for aluminium scrap; later on to Brookside Metal Company to store salvaged marine scrap. Hoppy survived the war but died a year or so afterwards.

On the twenty-fifth of July 1950, Mrs Hopkinson applied for permission to use the mill for mixing, packing and storing dyestuff.

She had become quite a leading character in the village, founding the first W.I. group, reviving the village Toc H, and playing a lively part in all the social activities of the people. It was she who renamed the mill house Corville House - a name she composed by using the first part of her Christian name coupled to the last part of her maiden name. After she and her son left the mill house it stood empty until it was pulled down in 1959 to widen the main road through the village.

In 1951 the Chapman brothers, Ernest and Stan, acquired the property. They were engineers and scrap-merchants. They made an application in June 1952 to use the premises for business purposes. A part of the mill was still in use for mixing and storing dyestuff. A man named John Allen came every weekday morning to work there. He started early and the Chapmans, who lived in St. Albans, gave him a key to let himself in. One morning Ernest Chapman drove to the mill

Stan & Earnest Chapman showing the front view of the old mill just before its demolition in 1984

Corville Mill. The new mill built as offices to replace the old Park Street Mill.

and found John Allen sitting outside, white faced and in a state of agitation.

'What's up?' Ernest called, as he got out of the car.

'There's a ghostly figure wandering all about in there making curious noises,' John told him. From then on, every morning, he'd wait for Ernest to turn up before attempting to open the door. Curiously enough, the description he gave of the figure could well have fitted the last of the working millers, George Wheeler, better known to the villagers as 'Foghorn' because of his terrific voice. John Allen had only recently come to the village and knew nothing about him, so his fright remained quite a mystery.

Bomb found ... but Ernie works on!

COOL-HEADED scrap boss Ernest Chapman hardly batted an eyelid when he discovered an unexploded naval mine dangling on the end of his crane.

It surfaced from under tons of discarded metal during a massive clear up at the Corville Mill site in Park Street.

But Mr Chapman, aged 76, had no idea his discovery would prompt a major police and army bomb disposal operation . . . 48 hours later.

After hooking up the five-feet long cylinder packed with explosives, he gently lowered it to the ground, propped it alongside other cylinders then amazingly he carried on working.

It was TWO days later before potential purchasers of the scrapyard site in Bury Dell Lane spotted the World War II relic and sounded the alarm.

"I was told it was just a gunpowder case. I just stood it on end with a lot

By
Chris Bristow

more cylinders. I suppose I should have realised," said Mr Chapman, of St Julians Road, St Albans.

He went on: "I don't suppose I'm very popular round here after half the houses were evacuated and even the pub was closed for a while."

Wednesday night's bomb scare ended without incident after two hours when bomb disposal experts removed the 1943 mine.

Added Mr Chapman: "It must have been there since 1951 when I bought the place. We never really bothered about what was in the far corner. It was just a heap of junk."

Article in dated

(Reproduced by kind permission)

In February 1984, Manto Properties Ltd, 60, London Road, Shenley, applied to get the mill listed and to make certain structural changes to it. Not long after the application Ernest Chapman began to clear away some scrap that had been dumped in the garden near the smithy during the last war and discovered an unexploded bomb.

In June that same year Jarvis Development Company of Harpenden obtained a contract to convert the mill to office use. Before the work started the Chapman brothers had two photographs taken of themselves showing the front and back of the old mill. During the rebuilding process some of the foundation timbers of previous mills were found deep in the mud beneath it in a splendid state of   preservation. An old key was also discovered and presented to Cyril H. Martin by Mr. Arnold of the Jarvis company.

Two semi-detached houses with garages have been erected on the site of the old smithy. They have been named Mill Cottages numbers one and two. At the time of writing a family named Harris occupies number one and the Jones family live in number two.

CHAPTER 4

THE ANCIENT PROPERTY OF MOOR MILL,
PAST AND PRESENT

We are not aware precisely when the first mill was built on this site. We do know that it pre-dates the mill further up the river originally named Parkye Mill, which was built by the Norman abbots about the middle of the 12th century. The fact that the mill here was taken over by Normans and mentioned in the Domesday Book means that it had a previous Saxon owner, but there is no record of how long it had been under Saxon influence. At that time Hertfordshire was part of Mercia and this particular part came under the control of the Abbey and Monastery at St. Albans, which dates back to the time of King Offa, having been founded in the year 793. The Domesday Book states that there was a mill here, on this part of the River Ver, controlled by the Saxon Manor of Hanstead (Hanamstede). In those times large areas of land, such as shires, were governed directly by the king, who held a court called a witon or gemot. Smaller areas, called hundreds were governed by an earl or a sheriff at a court known as a wapentake.

The ordinary villeins (people holding land or houses from the earl) met him or his overseer at a place central to the particular hundred, often just a conspicuous oak tree or other well known feature of the district, such as a mill. The villeins and other less privileged residents, such as bordars or cottars were not allowed to leave the manor. Those unhappy ones that did stray to obtain work, or for family reasons, became classified as 'fugitives' and suffered severe penalties.

Hanstead must have been a very attractive manor in 1086 for it held twenty-six villeins and three cottars as fugitives from the manor of Shenley. If a mill did exist here at the time of the first Anglo-Saxon settlement, it would have had to defend its rights from invading

Norsemen who attacked, burnt and pillaged many houses along the Watling Street less than a quarter of a mile away. Indeed, quite recently, within forty yards from the site of Park Biri manor house, charred remains of a body and a timber boat were found.

Once Christianity had been established, much of the Kingdom of Mercia, of which this is a part, passed from secular hands to those of the Church. During the Saxon occupation, important buildings such as manor houses and mills were set up by a central control, in this case the Monastery of St. Albans. The local lord of the manor had the power to extract rents for the tenancy of mills and fields. They were usually paid in kind, and a fixed proportion went to the upkeep of the monastery. Details of the fees, fines, rents and conditions of tenancy can be found in the Anglo-Saxon Chronicle in the British Library, London.

After the Conquest the Normans began to assess the 'worth' of their new kingdom. In 1086 when the accounts of the Domesday Book became available the Norman Abbot of St. Albans Monastery, to whom this district had been given, must have realised that many changes would be necessary to support a large monastery and its staff. One of the changes decided upon was to make the mills and waterways more profitable.

During the terms of office of the first five Norman abbots, from Paul de Caen to Robert de Gorham, just over a hundred years, Moremyll had to be partly altered and its water courses widened and deepened. About that time a record in the Park Court book (1237-1460) carried information that eighteen offenders were punished for hunting in the Abbot's woods and twenty-one for poaching fish of various kinds in his waters (all rivers and ponds or lakes). One offender was captured several times poaching trout in the Ver at Moremyll. The control of the mill had, apparently, passed from Hanstead to the Manor of Park. In 1330, during the term of office of the 15th Norman Abbot Richard de Wallingford, further structural changes were made and recorded which

23

improved the building and millterre. Richard, the son of a blacksmith, probably gave some of those changes his personal touch.

A few years later John Moote (Abbot from 1349 to 1396) rebuilt both Parkye Mill and Moremyll at a recorded cost of £22. He also rebuilt the Manor House of Parkye or Park Biri just across the Watling Street from the mill. During his term of office the more densely populated parts of the manor had been decimated by the Black Death. The mills and less populated areas were not so badly affected.

Obviously, as the overall population was so reduced, dues and taxes had to be raised in order to maintain the monastery income. As far as the mills were concerned, that meant raising the toll for grinding corn or increasing the cost of the licence which allowed the people to use their own querns. Any fines or punishments arising out of these actions were settled in court by an action known as Suite at Mill. There is no doubt that the burden of the new taxes would have been peacefully tolerated had not the Abbot included another range of taxation and punishments which affected the burghers and other people of the district who had hitherto enjoyed a much higher standard of living. They organised themselves and an attack was made on the monastery. Other regions of the country were involved and finally a widespread uprising occurred under Wat Tyler in 1381 which resulted in the historical Peasants' Revolt.

One advantage of holding the tenancy of Moremyll after it had been rebuilt was the lifting of the constraint on fishing. Permission was granted, at that time, for the miller to use his own lines, nets or traps to catch various fish and eels in the waters adjacent to the mill, providing that he sent a regular supply to the monastery table. In fact eels became such a popular dish at the monastery that it wasn't long before they became the sole rent the miller was asked to pay.

After the Act of Supremacy of 1559 King Henry gave most of the church lands to those nobles who had gained his favour during the first part of his turbulent reign. Of course most of the poor parishioners were no better off under the new regime than they had been under the monastery.

From the time of the Dissolution until 1631 Quarter Sessions were held for the district at the Great Gateway in St. Albans. At each Easter Session wages for the various types of work were fixed and then held for the following year. Millers who were bachelors during that time were paid by the year, earning forty-six shillings and eightpence plus a pair of boots. The married ones earned fourpence a day with keep. Most skilled workers around the fields could earn up to eight-pence a day.

The Sessions Court often meted out very severe punishment for current 'criminal' offences. One could be hanged for burglary. Curiously enough, escape from the extreme penalty was often possible if the offender claimed that he could read. Many got away by learning by rote a passage from the Bible that had become the standard test.

Before the dissolution of the Monastery of St. Albans it was the custom for any miller who died at Moremyll to leave most of his possessions for disposal at the Manor of Park Biri. In 1529, however, a law was passed by the government which called for an inventory to be made of a deceased tenant's goods and chattels if they were of a value of five pounds or over.

The local history society of Bricket Wood has recently published a book entitled *All My Worldly Goods* which gives information concerning wills, inventories and administrative bonds of many local people in Bricket Wood, Park Street, and Chiswell Green during the years 1447 to 1715. From that book the names Beldon, Pruden, Marlborough and Fuller appear as occupants of Moormill from 1670 to 1735.

They were followed by three generations of the Woodward family who held the mill until 1845. Information about them had to come from Margaret Young, a relative in Australia, who holds the family Bible which had been sent out to Victoria, Australia, about the time of the gold rush there. An extract from Margaret's letter follows:

As a young girl I was fascinated by the faded writing [in the family Bible] and intrigued by the names 'Moor Mill', 'St. Stephens', 'St. Peters' etc.

I know it was a great thrill for my mother that I visited these places in 1982/83, and indeed so exciting that 'Moor Mill' was still standing. Unfortunately my mother died in 1985. I know how interested she would have been to learn of the restoration of the mill, and of the history you are to write.

You mention your discovery of 9 other Woodwards, including William Woodward 1547 and Thomas Woodward 1726. I don't know how these relate to our family.

The original owner of our old Bible was Richard Simpson (1728-1796), so 1728 is as far back as the Bible entries take us. Richard's son-in-law was James Woodward of Moor Mill. I have enclosed a brief summary of the family tree information obtained from the entries in the Bible, up to Thomas Norris Woodward, miller (1830-1887), who came out to live in Australia.

The Woodwards were followed by a family named Cook, Alfred and Ebenezer. They had occupancy until the mill came up for sale by auction in 1875. The sale took place at the Peahen Hotel in St. Albans. Some of the documents concerning that sale are reproduced at the end of the book.

Readers of my book *An Edwardian Village and its People* will recognise Tom Gee, the purchaser, as one of the principal characters mentioned. One of Tom Gee's daughters, Ethel Louisa, was a gifted and enterprising woman. She took a great interest in the business affairs of the mill and her father's employees and eventually married one of them named Leonard Alfred Page Taylor. After her father died she and her

26

husband purchased the freehold of the mill and most of its farmland. The fields nearest to the mill were largely engaged in raising cattle and poultry. They also bred pigs for market; this was known as 'pig-higgling'. They started a milk delivery business from a small shop in Park Street - originally a cabinet-maker's shop.

In 1932 they employed a former miller and brewer named Ronald Bragg who came from Balsam in Cambridgeshire to run the mill. He remained there until 1942 when essential war-work was required of him. Other employees at that time were the brothers Walter and Bibby Howlett, Frank Humbles and a stockman named Wisbey who lived in one of the mill cottages. The milk delivery service was efficiently run by a young girl named Rene Baldwin who eventually married Bibby Howlett.

Geoff (Leonard Taylor's son) and his wife Jean took over the mill and all its business activity after the death of his father. While living at the old mill house two daughters were born to them, followed a few years later by twins, a boy and a girl. Sometime before 1965 Inns & Company had acquired the right to extract minerals from some of the mill lands. In the early part of that year an agreement was signed between them and Geoff Taylor allowing him to contin-

The old cottages which fronted "The Street" were demolished in 1959. They faced the builder's yard. Here is Mrs. Howlett with her daughter and grandchild in the doorway of her roadside cottage. Most of these cottages had doors in two halves, similar to the old mill.

ue farming until digging operations began.

In 1919 Geoff's mother had purchased two small cottages standing on the river bank opposite The Red Lion pub in Park Street. After her husband's death, she sold one of them to Ronald Bragg her previous employee, to be used as a motor insurance office. He later bought the other one. The business that he started there still exists with a new owner and new premises. It was formerly a grocer's shop in Park Street, standing next door to Holy Trinity Church.

MOREMYLL
List of Tenants and Owners
A.D. 800 - 1989

800-1066	Lord of the Manor of Hanstead, owner.
1399	John Moote (Abbot of St. Albans), owner.
1401	John Wyndsor, owner.
1529-1542	John Redwood, tenant.
1670	John and Elizabeth Beldon, tenants.*
1686	Abraham Pruden, tenant.*
1722	Briant Marlborough, tenant.*
1735	William Fuller, tenant.*
1769	John Woodward, tenant.
1770-1800	James Woodward, tenant.
1800-1845	Thomas Woodward, tenant.
1845-1874	Alfred Cook, tenant.
1874-1875	Ebenezer Cook, tenant.
1875-1923	Tom Gee, tenant.
[1878]	{Freehold conveyance - J.J. Gape & G.G.T. Treherne to W. Phelps & Ors}
[1920]	{Freehold conveyance - Capt. W.N.W. Gape to L.A.P. Taylor}
[1923]	{Freehold conveyance - Trinity College, Oxford & Sidney Sussex College, Cambridge, to L.A.P. Taylor.}
1923-1944	L.A.P. Taylor, owner.
1944-1965	G. Taylor, owner.
1965-1980	G. Taylor, tenant. Inns & Co. 286 Pentonville Rd. London, landlord.
1980-1984	Department of Transport, owner.
1984-1989	Joe Carter, owner.
1989-	Reconstruction by Regents Inns (restaurant bar)

* Information from the book *All My Worldly Goods* by Meryl B. Parker and Bricket Wood History Society.

AGREEMENT, 13th October, 1908, between Baron Rendlesham (Fred Will Brook Thelluson) and Thomas Gee (landlord and tenant).

Clause 14. Tenant shall not at any time dig clay, gravel or sand from any part of said premises or make open pits.

Clause 11. Shall not erect or permit erection of advertisement boards on any building, posts, rails or gates without landlord's consent.

Clause 20. Landlord may resume possession of any part of premises for purpose of building or making roads at any time by compensation of an arbitrary amount.

LANDLORD includes heirs, successors and assigns.

TENANT includes executors, administrators and assigns.

Witness: Thomas Haton, Rendlesham Estate Official, Woodbridge.

COLNEY STREET FARM

Loc'n	Title		A R P	Vicar £ s d	Lomax £ s d
539	Little Roger Mead	Grass	1 1 33	1 4	
584	Cow Meadow	Grass	5 2 25	10 3	1 0 4
585	Roger Mead Grazing	Grass	7 1 19	10 10	1 5 4
586	Water Dell Cross	Arable	5 2 31	4 1	-
587	Twelve Acres	Arable	12 1 14	4 2	3 10 10
588	Red Cow Field	Arable	8 1 34	9 5	2 6 6
589	Little Mill Field	Arable	3 3 36	5 3	1 3 10
600	New Orchard	Grass	4 0 14	1 0 1	0 8 2
601	Homestead	-	1 1 18	3 0	-
607	Orchard	Grass	3 1 28	1 1 0	6 10
607a	Plantation	-	0 1 11	-	-
608	Orchard Field	Arable	5 3 8	7 1	1 12 9
609	Mount Field	Arable	9 1 2	10 3	2 4 9
610	Saw Pit Bd.	Arable	7 3 28	8 6	2 2 8
611	Wiggs Meadow	Grass	3 2 24	5 7	17 2
	River	-	0 2 26	-	-
			81 1 21	6 0 10	16 19 2

AGREEMENT 13th October, 1908

between

Baron Rendlesham

and

Thomas Gee

Field Schedule

Ord. Map No.	Description	A	R	P	location	Plan
Pt 223	Bldgs. Cottages No.					
	22 & 23 with gardens	0	2	9	3	
216	Orchard	4	3	15	3	
210	Orchard	3	1	2	3	
212	Pasture	8	0	34	3	
213	Pasture	3	3	0	3	
263	Pasture	3	2	8	2	
556	Pasture	7	0	20	1	
366	Pasture	2	2	8	2	
265	Pasture	3	2	28	2	
558	Pasture	0	0	11	1	
559	Pasture	1	0	26	1	
570	Arable	4	0	26	1	
549	Arable	7	3	13	1	
550	Arable	21	3	15	1	
563	Arable	12	1	2	1	
368	Arable	11	2	18	2	
360	Arable	11	1	4	2	
264	Arable	26	0	10	1	
211	Arable	15	2	19	3	
554	Water	2	0	37	1	
557	Water	0	1	23		1
Let for a yearly rent of £160		152	0	8		

31

Entries from the family Bible of Margaret Young,
Great grand-daughter of *Thomas Norris Woodward

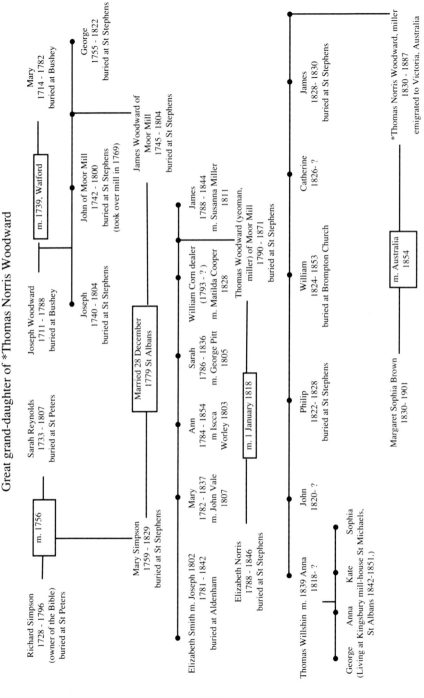

Back of cost sheet

G.H. Gibson's prices from Booker Kiln per 1000:

		s	d
Wycombe High Bricks	..	6	0
Wycombe West Bricks	..	6	0
Daws Hill Bricks	..	4	0
Sand Pit			
Wycombe High	..	2	0
Wycombe West	..	2	0
Daws Hill	..	1	9
Lime			
Wycombe High	..	3	0

Front of cost sheet

For Horses

Condition Powders (Barretts recipe)

1/4 lb Elecampane powder
1/4 lb Gentian powder
1/4 lb Fenugreek powder
1/2 oz Coriander seed powder
1/2 oz Steel of Antimony
1/2 oz Liver of Antimony
1/2 oz Brimstone
1/2 oz Nitre
One tablespoonful in damp food at night.

MOOR MILL,

BETWEEN

ST. ALBANS & RADLETT, HERTS,

17 miles from London.

PARTICULARS, WITH PLANS AND CONDITIONS OF SALE,

OF THE VALUABLE

WATER CORN MILL,

WITH SUBSTANTIALLY - BUILT

DWELLING HOUSE,

KNOWN AS

MOOR MILL,

AND CONVENIENT

FARM BUILDINGS, YARDS

AND

34 ACRES

OF PRODUCTIVE

MEADOW & ARABLE LAND,

BETWEEN

ST. ALBANS AND RADLETT,

FOR SALE BY AUCTION, BY

MR. RUMBALL,

AT THE PEAHEN HOTEL, ST. ALBANS,

On FRIDAY, JULY 30th, 1875, at Two for Three o'clock,

IN ONE LOT.

May be viewed by permission of the tenant; and Particulars obtained of Messrs. GADSDEN & TCEHERNE, Solicitors, 2s, Bedford Row; and of Mr. RUMBALL, Land Agent and Surveyor, &c., Saint Albans.

GIBBS AND BAMFORTH, PRINTERS, ST. ALBANS.

34 ACRES

OF EXCELLENT

MEADOW AND ARABLE LAND,

Extending for nearly a mile by the side of the River,

In the following Enclosures :—

No.	Name of Field.	State.		Quantity.	
			A.	B.	P.
580	Mill Field	Arable	11	1	1
581	Cow Meadow	Grass	10	3	1
582	Hither ditto	Ditto	5	3	39
583	House, Mill, and Yards	Homestead	0	2	36
583a	Small Meadow	Grass	1	2	2
584a	Orchard	Ditto	0	1	27
616	Lane Meadow	Ditto	2	0	13
	River	. . . .	1	1	16
			34	0	15

Copyhold to 1 Manor of Pa

3.1.29 Freehold

. Let to Mr. Alfred Cook, as yearly tenant in the usual way, at a Rental of

£255 PER ANNUM.

Of the above, 3a. 1r. 29p. or thereabouts are of Freehold Tenure ; the rest is Copyhold of the Manor of Park, and subject to a Quit Rent of £0 19s. 8d., and the whole of the property is subject to a Land Tax of £10. 5s. 0d. per annum.

The Timber and Fixtures are valued at £95 10s. 0d., to be paid for in addition to the purchase money.

The present tenant, who has held the Mill for nearly 30 years, has, during that time, done an extensive business as Miller and Corn Dealer, and there being no other Mill down stream within 6 miles, and a fine head of water extending up stream for a considerable distance, with two flood gates and regulating fall, the Mill may be kept in constant work, and being within easy distance of several good market Towns, and 1½ miles of two Railway Stations, and 17 miles from London, there is every facility for doing an extensive trade.

CONDITIONS OF SALE

1.—No person shall advance less than £   at a bidding, and no bidding shall be retracted. Subject to the right the vendors hereby reserve to bid by their agent or agents as often as they please, the highest bidder shall be the purchaser, and if any dispute arise respecting a bidding, the property shall be put up again for re-sale.

2.—The purchaser shall, immediately after the sale, pay a deposit of £10 per cent. of his purchase money into the hands of the auctioneer, and sign an agreement in the annexed form to complete his purchase according to these conditions.

3.—The remainder of the purchase money and the value (as stated in the particulars) of the timber and fixtures shall be paid, and the purchase completed on the 29th day of September next, at the offices, No. 28, Bedford Row, London, of Messrs. Gadsden and Treherne, the vendors' solicitors, and if from any cause whatever the purchase shall not be completed on that day, the purchaser shall pay to the vendors interest after the rate of £5 per cent. per annum on the remainder of the purchase money until the completion of the purchase. The purchaser shall be entitled to the receipt of the rents and profits of the property from the said 29th day of September next, all outgoings up to that day being cleared by the vendors, and all current rents and outgoings shall be apportioned (if necessary) for the purposes of this condition.

4.—An abstract of the vendors' title will be delivered or sent as requested by the purchaser or his agent, within 14 days after the day of sale, and except so far as any delay may be occasioned by the vendors or their solicitors, the 15th day succeeding the day of sale shall be deemed the day of the delivery of the abstract.

5.—The title shall commence with the will dated the 12th day of June, 1822, of James Carpenter Gape, who died in the year 1827, and the purchaser shall assume that the testator was, at the date of his will, and continued from thence to the time of his death, seized in fee simple at the common law, and by the custom respectively of all the property offered for sale, and shall not require the production of, or investigate, or make any objection or requisition in respect of, the prior title, whether such prior title appear by recital, statement, or otherwise, or do not appear at all.

6.—The vendors shall not be liable to abstract, produce, or procure the production for any purpose of any muniments of title not in their possession or in that of the mortgagees, and if the purchaser shall require any deed or document to be stamped, or any attested, official, or other copies of or extracts from any muniments of title, whether or not in the vendors' possession, or any statutory or other declarations, certificates, or other evidence in support of the title, or in proof of identity, or of births, deaths, marriages, or other things, he shall obtain or procure the same respectively at his own expense.

7.—The purchaser shall not require any evidence of the identity of the property as described in the particulars, with the property described in the abstracted documents, other than such is afforded by a comparison of the description in the particulars and documents, together with a statutory declaration, which will be furnished to the purchaser, if he requires it, at his own expense, that the property has been held consistently with the title shewn by the abstract since the death of the above-named testator in the month of February, 1827. The vendors shall not be required to distinguish the copyhold from the freehold part of the property, and the purchaser shall not make any objection to the title on that account.

8.—The property is believed and shall be taken to be correctly described as to quantity and otherwise, and is sold subject to all chief and other rents, rights of way, water, and other easements (if any) charged or subsisting thereon, and to the existing tenancy. And if any error, misstatement, or omission in the particulars be discovered, the same shall not annul the sale, nor shall any compensation be allowed by the vendors in respect thereof.

9.—All objections and requisitions in respect of the title, or the abstract, or particulars, or anything appearing therein respectively, shall be stated in writing and sent to the vendors' solicitors within 14 days from the delivery of the abstract, (time being in respect of such 14 days of the essence of the contract), and all objections and requisitions not sent within that time, shall be considered to be waived. If any objection or requisition shall be made which the vendors shall be unable or unwilling to remove or comply with, the vendors shall be at liberty (notwithstanding any intermediate negotiation on the subject of such objection or requisition, or attempts to remove or comply with the same), by notice in writing to the purchaser to rescind the sale, in which case the purchaser shall receive back the deposit without interest, but shall have no claim on the vendors for the expenses of investigating the title or other expenses, or for compensation.

10.—Upon payment of the residue of the purchase money and the value of the timber and fixtures at the time and place above mentioned, the vendors and all other necessary parties will make and execute a proper surrender and assurance to the purchaser, but such surrender and assurance, and every other assurance and act (if any) which shall be required by the purchaser for getting in, surrendering, or releasing any outstanding estate, right, title, or interest, or for completing, or perfecting the vendors' title, or for any other purpose, shall be prepared, made, and done, by and at the expense of the purchaser, and every such assurance shall be left not less than 10 days before the said 29th day of September next at the offices aforesaid. The vendors are trustees selling under a trust for sale, and the concurrence of the parties beneficially interested shall not be required, and the purchaser shall not be entitled to any other covenants than several covenants by the vendors and other conveying parties that they respectively have not incumbered.

11.—Such muniments of title in the possession of the vendors as relate to other property, or to the proceeds of the sale, shall be retained by the vendors, who will enter into the usual covenant with the purchaser for the production and furnishing copies to him of the same, but such covenant shall be limited so as to bind the vendors personally so long only as they shall respectively have the custody of the said muniments, and the deed containing such covenant shall be prepared by and at the expense of the purchaser.

LASTLY.—If the purchaser shall fail to comply with these conditions, his deposit-money shall be forfeited to the vendors, who shall be at liberty to proceed to another sale, either by public auction or private contract, with or without notice to the purchaser at the present sale, and the deficiency, if any, occasioned by such second sale, together with all charges attending the same, shall immediately after such sale be made good by the defaulter at this present sale, and in case of non-payment of the same the whole shall be recoverable by the vendors as and for liquidated damages, and it shall not be necessary for the vendors to tender a conveyance.

37

CHAPTER 5

MEMORIES OF A LIVELY MOORMILL

1913-1918

At least once a week, just before and during the Great War, I used to walk to Moormill from my home in Park Street to buy rabbit food. We kept chickens and rabbits to eke out our scanty meat ration. I often accompanied other village boys who were on a similar errand. Sometimes my friend Gordon Drennan would join us but he wanted skimmed milk. His mother was a Scot and could make delectable Scotch scones with it. Our path led us across the village squire's private golf-links to follow the right bank of the river. Halfway to the mill, alongside the river bank, were some water-cress beds, fed by a cool spring which bubbled down from a part of the mill farmland known as Upper Grounds. We would separate at the mill, Gordon would take his milk can to the mill house while we went over the mill-race bridge and through a heavy wooden door into the place where the miller weighed and served us with our toppings or bran. The miller at that time was a Mr Hart who lived at Colney Street. He had a typical 'miller's thumb' - stumpy and worn smooth as silk by constantly testing flour.

We could see the water-wheels from where we waited. There were two of them which drove some huge gear-wheels and lengths of shafting. The grindstones were worked directly by the gears downstairs and upstairs. Other machines could be set in motion by long wooden 'striker-arms' which slid their belts on to the shafting. A chain pulley could be activated in the same way to lift heavy objects like sacks of corn up to the top floor. Other machines sifted or sorted produce from the farm or chopped it into cattle or pig food. Down below was a wood-burning stove which heated air for drying the grain. Several fans driven from the shafting forced the air through a series of wooden ducts to where it was needed to dry or winnow the grain. In those days the place was a real hive of industry. When the clean, dry corn was shovelled into the hoppers with large wooden shovels and the grinding began, the noise became deafening. The men in the carts below, waiting under the chain lifts, had to shout at the top of their voices so that Mr Hart could hear when they were ready for the sacks to be hauled up.

We boys liked to watch the men going about their various tasks. One particular product of the mill fascinated us. Horse beans were grown in the fields and they came to the mill to be processed. They were cooked, roasted and dried to end up a brown chocolate colour. They tasted almost as good as chocolate too. We called them 'locusts'. Out schoolteacher told us they were what John the Baptist fed on in the wilderness. Sweets were in short supply during the Great War and we often helped ourselves from the bin where the 'locusts' were kept.

Not only was the mill very busy during those years but so too were the men working in the surrounding fields. There was always work for several men ploughing, sowing and reaping as well as looking after cows and pigs. Of course most of the heavy work was done by horses at that time. One labourer had an all-the-year-round job cutting the hedges and clearing the weeds along the waterways to the mill.

On the way home we would often stop for a drink of water from the spring near the watercress beds. An exciting thing happened there during the last war. A Handley Page bomber returning to the aerodrome just across the Watling Street developed engine trouble and 'pancaked' right into the watercress beds.

A suitable epitaph to the last of the millers would be the following verse, once used as a popular ballad and sung and acted during Victorian party games. It was called the Jolly Miller. With

39

apologies to the 17th century author for my change of words.

There was a miller-farmer once

Whose name was Thomas Gee

He farmed the land and ground the corn

As happy as could be.

If things went wrong, he sang this song

A really quaint dit-tee

"I care for nobody, no not I

And nobody cares for me.

I care for nobody, no not I

And nobody cares for me."

View south from the mill, 1908. Public house on the right is the Falcon with the entrance to Park Street Lane just beyond.

(*above*) View facing north, 1910, showing the mill house on the corner of Burydell Lane. Mrs. Cook is on the right and Dorie Cook standing in the street

View showing the White Horse pub and the builder's yard. The giant horse chestnut tree was the meeting place for the villagers for hundreds of years. On the right is the entrance to Park Valley farmhouse and yard.

41

1954, looking south from The Swan public house. On the left are the 16th century beamed cottages standing between two sections of the mill front garden wall. The old mill house stands further down, at the curve of the road on Burydell corner.

CHAPTER 6

SMITHS AND WORKERS IN IRON

The smithy and casting shop at the mill in Park Street was taken over by the Martin family of smiths about the time the mill was held by Richard Francklyn. William and Elizabeth Martin came to Park Street from the Abbey district of St. Albans where two of their boys were registered - Will, born in 1687 and Joseph in 1689. From that time the men of the family carried on working at the mill workshop throughout five generations. As well as casting various pieces of hardware for the mill, they made hard-wearing farmers' equipment such as plough-tips, roller-rings, pulleys and weights. In addition they cast hinges, bolts, door-knockers and door-handles for the local builders; also many kinds of garden and household fittings, such as foot-scrapers. Some of the door-knockers and foot-scrapers survived into the 20th century.

It is quite possible that the Martins took over one of the three ancient cottages standing on the mill grounds near the workshop.

Records show that there was a wheelwright named Ingram and a water worker named Seabrook employed on the mill property. Those families could have occupied the other two cottages as there was another record of Joseph Martin's son, also called Joseph, marrying a Sarah Ingram. They had a daughter Susannah, who married a John Seabrook in 1757. People didn't travel far in those days to find a suitable marriage partner. Anyway, that particular branch of the Martins died out.

Joseph's elder brother Will, born in 1687, married an Elizabeth Jenkins on April 22nd, 1717. One of their children, named after his father, was born on March 6th, 1719.

When old Will died in 1727 his wife leased the White Horse farm and the family probably left the cottage and went to live at the farmhouse. Young Will, however, continued to work at the mill with his cousin and uncle Joseph. In February 1740 he married Elizabeth Robinson. A son was born to them on July 4th, 1756, whom they named George. On Sunday, 11th January, 1789, George married Mary Quick, daughter of the publican at the Blackboy, a public-house near Garston. They had a family of three sons and three daughters. The eldest son, George (born 1792), married an Elizabeth Godman on August 22nd, 1813. She came from a family well known in the district as engineers and surveyors. They had fourteen children in all, including two sets of twins. Five girls were born before the first son, George, 'turned up' in 1822. He was the last of the five generations of Martins to work at the mill workshop. When the Beament family came to the village and started rebuilding the mill, George and Elizabeth moved to a smithy in Chiswell Green, where they started an alehouse at a nearby cottage.

The Blacksmith Tradition

The last of the Martin family's forge in Leavesdon demolished when Rolls Royce extended their aerodrome.

With the passing of years a tradition had developed in the Martin family, that at least one son of each new generation would set out to start another business. After old George died in 1844 his brother Will (born 1796) took over the smithy and alehouse at Chiswell Green; while another brother (born September 1798) who had been named Isaac after his mother's father Isaac Quick, became the village black-smith at Elstree. The smithy there is still in use today, producing many types of wrought-ironwork. Young George married Susannah Higham in 1845 and they came to Park Street and

took over The Swan Inn. George had a brother named Thomas, born February 1826, who started a smithy attached to the Harrow public house in Verulam Road, St. Albans. Some years later Thomas converted it into a cycle shop.

After George and Susannah became proprietors of The Swan, the construction of the railway line from Watford to St. Albans was begun. A part of Lovetts farm, on which The Swan stood, was taken by the London and North Western Railway

Company. It had to be banked-up fifteen to twenty feet above the level of the field. During that operation there must have been much coming and going of workmen and L. & N.W. railway officials into and around the pub, which evidently nurtured a close relationship between all these people and George Martin, the publican, because

George was asked to lay the 'key-brick' in the arch spanning the main road. Another product of that association was that a great deal of railway timber and other material came to be used in the construction of his new blacksmith's shop.

The only parts of the old mill workshop that were worth installing in the new one were the bellows and feed-pipes which, surprisingly enough and despite their antiquity, were in fairly good working order. Obviously they had been refurbished from time to time. Some time after his father's death in 1844 George decided to leave The

Swan and start another business at Garston near his grandmother's people, leaving his young brother Alfred in charge of the new smithy in Burydell Lane, Park Street. At the time of his departure The Swan Inn had a front garden separated from
the main road by a wooden fence. There was a path leading to the front door with flower beds on each side. George's granddaughter Kate Martin had a picture of it hanging on her sitting-room wall at 95, Cecil Street, Watford.

The Garston Forge
George Martin's grandmother had been a member of the Quick family. Her relations lived at Trowley Bottom, a tiny hamlet not far from Garston. They lived next door to a family named Ashby.

Along Horseshoe Lane at Garston there were some cottages which had a considerable garden space. George took one of the cottages and set up a smithy backing on to the wall of the garden. Further along the lane, which led to Leavesden, stood All Saints church. After his death in 1891 George was buried there beside a number of his relations. That part of the churchyard came to be known as Martins Corner.

George had three sons at the time of moving: George Henry (born 1846), Albert (born 1851) and Frederick (born 1854). In 1874 Albert married Sarah Ashby, whose family had been living next door to the Quicks. They had five children. Albert carried on working at the Garston forge after his father died and was, for many years, Sexton at All Saints church. About a decade ago, the Martin forge was extracted from its Garston site and re-erected as a show-piece at the Chiltern Open Air Museum near Chalfont St. Giles.

Frederick Martin started another blacksmith's shop at Leavesden and became a very notable character in the district. The following is an extract from the obituary which appeared in the Watford

46

Observer just after his death in 1943.

THE LATE MR. FREDERICK MARTIN

We regret to record the death of Mr. Frederick Martin which took place at his home 'Rosebank' Leavesden on Wednesday at the age of 89 years. The late Mr. Martin was actively engaged in public work. He was elected to Watford Rural District Council in December 1895, a year after its formation, remaining a member for over 40 years. In April 1919 he was elected to the Board of Guardians. Twice he was chairman of the Council and he was appointed a member of the Watford Guardians Committee on its formation. He retired in May 1937.

In 1926 Mr. Martin was appointed a Justice of the Peace and sat on the Watford Bench. He served for some years on the Watford Burial Board, being vice-chairman at one time, and was also a member of the Watford Joint Hospital Board. For many years he was vicar's warden at All Saints Church Leavesden. Other appointments he held were membership of the Old Age Pensions Committee, a trustee for Watford Church Lands, a trustee for the Reading Room, a manager of Leavesden Schools, and a worker for the Hospital Contributory Scheme.

In 1935 Mr. and Mrs. Martin celebrated their diamond wedding, when they were the recipients of two armchairs from the members of the Rural District Council. Also on that occasion they received telegrams of congratulation from King George V and Queen Mary, and many others from those people with whom he had worked in his official capacity. The Burial Board presented them with a radio set.

CHAPTER 7

THE RETURN TO PARK STREET

George and Susannah Martin's eldest son was about eleven when they moved to Garston. When he was old enough, George Henry followed the family tradition by leaving home, but instead of starting another business he went to work in the blacksmith's shop attached to Sedgewick's Brewery. At that time the brewery was owned by Lady Sedgewick. The founder of the firm, her husband, had been dead quite some time when George Henry went there to work. The brewery was one of the oldest, if not the oldest, in Watford and employed about 100 people. There were six blacksmiths at work there in the smithy. Later on, George Henry became the head blacksmith and also the leader of the brewery's famous fire brigade.

When his father died George Henry inherited the Park Street smithy. In 1899, when his uncle Alfred retired, he sent his son Herbert to Park Street to take care of the business. Herbert had worked a few years for his father at the brewery smithy, but before that he worked for a year or two as a clerk on the London and North Western Railway. It obviously took a few years to settle down as a blacksmith in the quiet rural village Park Street was in those days.

Teddy and Marky Beament occupied the mill at that time and Herbert paid the rent of the smithy to them, quite unaware of a family change of ownership. When Stanley Giddins came to live at the mill house Herbert did some work for him then put in a bill for £2.14.5. After payment was long overdue he sent another bill, but instead of a settlement he received a notice from Mr Giddins saying that all future rent for the smithy should to paid to him. That was on December 20th, 1906. Herbert went to see Teddy Beament who assured him that he must continue paying the rent to him and not to Stanley Giddins. So Herbert sent in another bill for his work. The only response was another notice for rent. Then two more bills came from the executors of Chaffy Giddin's will for back rent. After further discussions with the Beaments the situation became an impasse. As a last resort Herbert decided to take the matter to Court. After the case was settled a notice appeared in the *Herts Advertiser* as follows:

WHO IS THE LANDLORD?

Herbert Martin the blacksmith at Park Street sued Stanley Giddins the mill owner for £2.14.5 for work done. Giddins put in a counter-claim for £6 rent. Mr J.E. Ellis appeared for the plaintiff, Mr P. Griffith-Jones for the defendant.

At the opening of the case Mr Griffith-Jones admitted the claim subject to the counter claim, which, he said, was for the occupation of the blacksmith's shop in Park Street. The case arose because Mr Giddin's father, Chaffy Giddins owned property in Park Street which included the blacksmith's shop 'the matter in dispute'.

Chaffy Giddins died on May 1st, 1905. His executors put up all his property for sale by auction. That was in October 1905 and it was bought by Stanley Giddins 'the defendant in this action'. After the sale a claim was sent to the blacksmith for rent followed by two further claims after the estate had been conveyed on December 20th, 1906, that was the defendant's position. He had never been able to secure any rent.

At that stage Mr. Griffith-Jones explained the relationship between his client and the Beaments. Mr. Beament, he said, was brother-in-law of the late William Chaffy Giddins, and used, on his behalf, to collect the rents of the smithy and two cottages. He then deducted a portion of it for the service rendered. Before the property was sold Mr. Beament also collected the rent for the executors and they used to allow him to keep some of the rent against the interest on a thousand pounds which they had to pay him under the will of the late William Chaffy Giddins. Mr. Ellis replied and then put forward the case for the blacksmith. He said

49

that the smithy in question had been held for a great many years by the Martin family and they had always paid the rent to the Beament family. It was true that Mr. Martin had received a notice to pay rent to Mr. Giddins, but he had also received an express notice from Mr. Beament, whom he had always regarded as the landlord, that he was not to pay anyone but him. In those circumstances what could he do? He paid Mr. Beament the rents and obtained receipts.

After a pause in the proceedings, during which his Honour was summing up the case, judgement was given for the plaintiff on the claim, and for the defendant on the counter claim: costs being allowed for the latter at a lower scale.

Obviously, no attempt had been made by Stanley Giddins or the Beament brothers to enlighten the blacksmith about the true facts of their claims because that would have given him an opportunity to pay his rent straight into Court. They would then have had to appear against each other in order to claim it. Anyway, the Beaments must have felt pretty sore about their part in the case because whenever Marky Beament met Herbert's son in the village street he would take out his metal purse and push out a penny to give him. When Herbert Martin heard about it and his son asked him why, adding 'he never gives one of the other boys one', Herbert gave him this cryptic answer which puzzled him for years: 'That's probably conscience money'. If that court case did nothing else, it caused the smithy to be put on the mill plans.

Soon after the Great War started, two contingents of artillery and signals came to the village. Many soldiers encamped on the Vicarage field, others were billeted at the villagers' homes. The blacksmith's shop was commandeered by an officer, staying at Frogmore House, for the use of army farriers and smiths. For upwards of a year the smithy had as many as six or eight army workers mending army vehicles and shoeing horses and mules.

After the local work had fallen to a few odd jobs Herbert Martin decided to close the smithy and join up. He had been disgusted with the way the army farriers hobbled the horses and shoed them lying on the ground so he went to a naval recruiting office and joined up as a sea-going engine-room artificer, spending the rest of the war years afloat. On his return to the village he found that the blacksmith's trade had suffered a severe set-back during his absence. Motor transport had almost completely replaced the horse and cart.

One of the first things he did was to convert his double forge into a single one. He removed the bellows and draught-pipes that his predecessors had been using for many years and replaced them with a modern rotary blower. He knew that his grandfather had moved the forge equipment from the workshop on the main road to the shop in Burydell but he was entirely unaware of its real antiquity. The iron parts were sold to a scrap merchant while the bellows lay around the back of the shop for a long while before being broken up.

I was fourteen years old at that time and worked for my father, Herbert Martin. I had been used to working the bellows ever since I was six. When the draught-pipes were removed I became interested in the curious lettering embossed on them.

The first big job the blacksmith obtained after the war was a contract with Ronald Beach Christmas to help convert the mill from a water-driven system to a completely different one driven by steam - a golden opportunity to exploit the experience gained in the Navy. After many months of hard work by the blacksmith and the local builder, Will Rentowl, who did the timber and brickwork, the ancient flour mill was finally converted into a steam-driven glue factory. Most of the Park Street villagers hated to see their flour mill, the metacentre of village life throughout the ages, disappear in that manner and were not at all pleased with the smell and appearance of its replacement. The factory went on producing glue for only a few years before Mr

Christmas decided to sell the property and use some of its equipment to start an entertainment centre in Bricket Wood.

The Great War had caused a mushroom growth of factories and workshops all over the country that were soon mass-producing volumes of the type of iron-work that had once been the prerogative of the blacksmith's craft. Practically the only forge-welding Herbert Martin did after the war consisted of a few ornamental gates, fire-baskets and screens of wrought iron, including customer-designed name-plates, weathercocks and hinged swinging signs. The business gradually developed into a supply and repair shop for motor-cycles, cycles and lawn mowers.

Such was the level of work going on at the Smithy, one day when Captain Hopkinson called to obtain his half year's rent, which had to be paid in advance, he told Herbert that his next payment would be raised to a sum nearly three times greater. Knowing the circumstances in which the smithy had come to be built there, Herbert told the mill owner that he would rather move out than pay that amount. 'This is all you own,' he added, pointing to the garden wall and the one near the river. 'The rest belongs to me.' As a result, when he paid the half-yearly rent, the blacksmith gave notice that he would vacate the premises in six months.

A few weeks before the termination of the notice Herbert Martin moved all of his equipment into a brand new smithy he had managed to get built at the head of the village, leaving the old one, a mere barn-like structure that one would never recognise as a black-smith's shop. The new smithy, in Hawfield Gardens, near the new railway bridge served Herbert Martin for the rest of his working days. It still stands there, in first-class order, converted into a bungalow when Herbert, the last of 300 years of Martin village blacksmiths, retired in about 1955.

My great-grandfather George Martin (born 1822) was living at The Swan (then an alehouse) in 1857 when the railway came. He left Park Street shortly afterwards to start a smithy at Garston, leaving his young brother Alf in charge of the forge at Park Street. The Martin's forge at Garston has now been excavated and re-erected in Buckingham at the Chiltern Open Air Museum, Newland Park.

In George Martin's time there was a cultivated garden between the alehouse at Park Street and the village street. By Edwardian times the garden had disappeared and the space was in use as a coal and coke yard kept by Phil Gilby, a cabinet maker. It was the first house on that side of the road as one entered the village. There was an old army hut in the garden and a great many village meetings and entertainments took place there. At the time of the book An Edwardian Village and its People it became the unofficial centre of village life and entertainment.

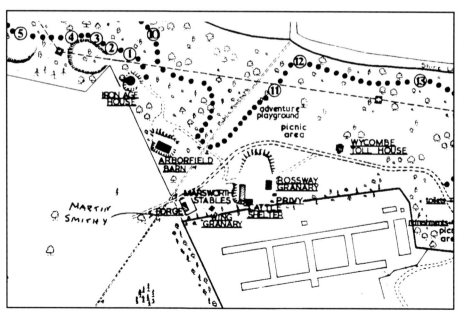

Sketch map of the current location of the Martin forge in the Chiltern
Open Air Museum, Chalfont St Peter, Buckinghamshire.

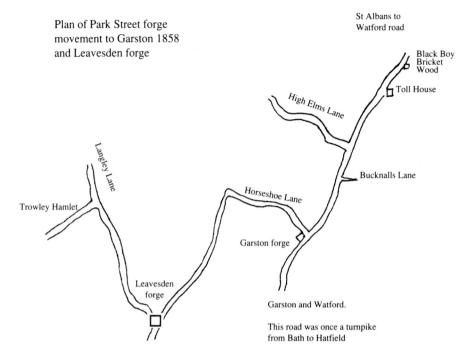

Plan of Park Street forge
movement to Garston 1858
and Leavesden forge

St Albans to
Watford road

Black Boy
Bricket
Wood

Toll House

High Elms Lane

Langley Lane

Bucknalls Lane

Trowley Hamlet

Horseshoe Lane

Garston forge

Leavesden
forge

Garston and Watford.

This road was once a turnpike
from Bath to Hatfield

54

EPILOGUE
A FOND FAREWELL TO A DYING CRAFT

So Time once more is the master and I'm sorry in a way
To part from my little smithy, where I've laboured many a day.
'Tis no architectural wonder, with historic relics rife
But it served a useful purpose, as I toiled along thro' life.

"A pavilion steeped in splendour" I'd never called it such
To me it was a haven that I cherished very much
For the clanging of the anvil was as music to my soul
That has sounded thro' the ages as long years onward roll.

'Twas never a work for weaklings, or those of a craven heart
Nor yet for a listless shirker who cannot buckle his part,
But men like Thor and Odin may still in a forge be found,
(Where signs of the old craft linger) by a leather apron bound.

Then, what are the main essentials to keep the standard high?
Muscles of spring-steel tension, quick hand and a dead-sure eye.
A mind that brooks no failure, of a right arm strong and true,
A measure of virtuous patience - a he-man through and through.

Great thuds of heavy sledge blows, oft made my anvil ring
I gloried in the music those hammer blows could bring
And the sparks that burst in brilliant rain to land upon the floor
Gave me a show of fireworks till they died to glow no more.

No crown of glory waiting, nor a ransom here to gain
But to be the lord of a smithy - what matters knocks and pain?
Deep brands of red-hot irons my hands and arms have borne,
I still bear scars of flesh-wounds a mule's sly kicks had torn.

There ne'er was a sordid moment, not any that I can tell,
For my work was often livened with many a joke as well.
A welcome eye to a passer-by, thro' smoke from a burning hoof,
And a word of praise in a voice that raised no echoes from the roof.

There'll be nothing to mark my going, no heralds in cloth of gold
Nor front page news in the paper, with headlines large and bold.
That would be flights of fancy, the things I never sought
The thanks that comes of doing well is a praise that can't be bought.

My limbs are becoming shaky and I'm more than a wee bit slow
So my story must be finished and now is the time to go -
But there's no other life like a blacksmith; let those deny who can.
Thank God I was called to do it - the work of a husky man.

[Composed for the 'passing' of Frank Reed, master blacksmith of
Digswell, by his daughter and his nephew. Frank learnt his trade at Park
Street but the poem refers to his ancient smithy at Digswell which he
discovered in the early twenties and worked there until his retirement.
Frank and his smithy figured largely in a film called 'The Queen of
Herts' made by the Welwyn Garden City Film Company.]

CHAPTER 8
SOME INTERESTING FEATURES OF ANCIENT RADLETT
AND ITS EARLY PROPRIETORS

Somewhere near the junction of the Aldenham-Shenley road and the Watling Street, in the heart of present day sprawling Radlett, once stood a cluster of thatched-roof timber cottages that were recorded in the early part of the 13th century under the name of Radwelleheved. The name passed through several changes in subsequent records until the 15th century, when it became Radelut and was interpreted to mean "road meeting place". The Romans might have found a few such dwellings when they came through in the 1st century A.D. laying down the foundations of Watling Street. They evidently found it a suitable place for some of them to stay and set up kilns for making pots. Their road ran parallel to a stream flowing roughly northwards, known today as The Brook. In those days it must have been a considerable watercourse, especially at the confluence with a smaller stream from Shenley where it turned in a northwesterly direction, for they took the trouble to construct a timber bridge there, similar to the one over the River Colne at Colney Street. The timber bridge was replaced by one of brick in 1745; marking a significant upsurge in local authority at that time, since such innovations had been held back by Clause 23 of the Magna Carta of 1215, which firmly stated that no community or individual should be compelled to make bridges over rivers except those who were legally bound, as of old, to do so.

In 1898, in the vicinity of Loom Lane, several Roman kilns were excavated and dated to have been in use during the 1st and 2nd century A.D. One of them, crammed full of half-baked pots in perfect condition. Some, carrying the potter's name Castus clearly marked, were found totally preserved in situ. A model of the kiln was made and put on show at Verulamium Museum, St. Michaels. The style of life of the kiln workers at Loom Lane went unrecorded but whatever it was it came to an abrupt end when Roman occupation ended in A.D. 410. Nor were other records kept of local events until the Saxon invasion three hundred years later.

About the year 700 A.D. Anglo-Saxon families made sporadic incursions into the district around Radwelleheved. They built timber houses, naming them after objects or people in their Saxon hierarchy, and surrounding them with moats for protection. Records remain of the following important places: the Overweld or Wyldhall, a house in the hamlet of Oakhurst that once existed near the present-day Wild Farm, and Sherlands, due west of those parts. Further south were two more houses, Bonesbushes and Kendals, recorded as belonging to the Manor of Tyteburst, an area extending along the valley of the River Tyke (an ancient name for The Brook). At the time the records were taken the land belonged to the Church. Kendals had been built by a certain Jordan de Kendal early in the 12th century, but the builder of Bonesbushes, much older, went unrecorded. Robert Sherland held Sherlands for the Abbot of Westminster in 1308. Kendals and Bonesbushes were in possession of the Abbot of St. Albans. Records show that rent for the manor in 1276 was eight days' work, thirty eggs, one cock, two hens, two capons, plus an annual presentation of lillyflowers to the Prioress of Markyate. Rojer le Porter held the Overwyld in 1320. Later the Porter family built a new house near the site of the old moated house and named it Porters; that, together with Sherlands was purchased in 1748 by a rich distiller and maltster named John Mason (buried in St. Botolphs, Shenley Churchyard).

Although for hundreds of years Park Street had been the centre of three important estates there had never been anyone actually living in the village who was important or wealthy enough to sponsor, guide and support its day-to-day activities, until King George the First came to the throne.

London was only twenty miles away, but the once-splendid Roman Roads had deteriorated into miles of muddy tracks, scarred and furrowed by the iron-clad wheels of horse-drawn stage-coaches, carts and the carriages of the well-to-do.

A vast number of the poorer classes were beginning to 'drown their sorrows' not by quantities of old English ale as had been their wont, but by a cheaper short drink with more fire in it, commonly known as gin, which came over from Holland about the time of Queen Anne.

Among the gentry living in the capital at that time, dwelt a wealthy family named Mason. Their fortune was due to this change in the poor people's drinking habits. They were distillers and maltsters in the City and had amassed a huge fortune by supplying this potent liquor to the public at large at a price it could afford. Many of the London pubs and 'doss-houses' put up notices, 'Drunk for a penny, dead drunk for tuppence, a bed of clean straw for nothing'.

Mason married the daughter of Field Marshal Wade who had devised a method of improving the roads, in an appalling state at that time, by rolling in a mixture of stones and clay with a heavy horse-drawn roller. Thus the roads were Wade-ised a long time before they became Macadamised. Was it sheer chance, I wonder, that the date Wade obtained his Road Charter (1745) coincided with the building of the new bridge over The Brook?

John Mason's son George was a writer and a personal friend of Lord Howe. He wrote a great number of historical works including *The Life of Richard, Lord Howe,* a copy of which is held in the Royal Collection at the British Museum.

Improvements in the roads encouraged many wealthy London merchants, property owners and business people to drive their carriages further and further into the surrounding countryside without fear of getting stuck in the mud. Many of them set out on the roads in search of a second home in which to spend week-ends away from the smoky atmosphere and the congested London streets; or even a permanent home for retirement.

Joseph Wigg was a Master of the Brick and Tile Manufacturing Company situated in Gray's Inn Lane, now known as Gray's Inn Road. He was also Surveyor to the Inner Temple. On one of his journeys he fell in love with an old house in the Parish of Aston, a few miles east of Hertford. He took it over, made some alterations, and called it Frogmore Hall.

Some years afterwards he drove down to Park Street and Frogmore and purchased two cottages there. About the latter end of the eighteenth century his son Francis was getting married and probably throught that Frogmore would be a suitable place in which to set up his new home. The ancient Manor of Park Biri or 'Parkye' had been split into two parts and the northern part, known as Park Valley Estate, came onto the market and Francis bought it. He built himself a house just opposite his father's cottages and came there to live in 1819.

Lord Howe purchased the Porter mansion and park, and George moved into Sherlands, renaming it Aldenham Lodge. It had been known as 'Randolphs' previous to that.

Admiral Lord Howe had fought many naval battles against the French during the Seven Years' War. His naval and military exploits in America during the War of Independence had become legendary. When not at sea he spent much of his time at Porters arranging a part of it in the style of his cabin on board the flagship 'Queen Charlotte'. George Mason died unmarried in 1806. The property had to come on to the market owing to the tragic death by drowning of George's two heirs. It was bought by Thomas Part in 1870. About 1902 the Part family founded Starveacres and Newlands to celebrate the end of the Boer War. In 1926 Charles T. Part sold the rest of the estate. Porters is commemorated by Porters Park Golf Course.

Bonesbushes (Alias Newberries, alias Organ Hall) passed from the Abbot of St. Albans to Sir Humphry Coningsby who purchased it in 1509. It was acquired about 1548 by Edward Briscoe whose mother was a Coningsby. The estate remained in the House of Briscoe until 1709. W. B. Phillimore inherited the property from his father but sold it in 1870 to Mr Thomas Bagnal who became a great benefactor to the village. He was succeeded by Sir Francis Head, a member of an ancient Kentish family. An heiress of the Head family married Moses Mendez, Court Physician to Charles the Second. The heraldic arms of the Mendez family were four unicorns and five broken shinbones over a motto Study Quiet. Although the subsequent offspring of the marriage bore the name of Head they were credited with the Mendez Arms which appear on the family tomb in Radlett churchyard. The father of Sir Francis, the first baronet, had been a Privy Councillor, a great traveller and a writer of some distinction.

Sir Francis himself had a tremendous zeal for privacy. He pulled down several cottages on Shenley Hill that bordered his estate and was often seen riding around on horseback checking that no trespassers encroached on his property. Just before he died (in August 1887) he expressed a wish that his remains be buried in a certain shrubbery on the estate. Although his dying wish was duly carried out, his widow, who died four months afterwards, left instructions that her husband's body be disinterred and re-buried alongside her own in the family tomb in Radlett burial ground which had been consecrated just a few days previously.

The estate passed to H.J. Lubbock (1830-1910) who was brother to the first Lord Avebury. Mr Lubbock was a sporting gentleman and keen on cricket. He converted a part of the extensive parkland into a cricket ground for the use of the village. In 1905 the property was purchased by Mr. George Miller (1839-1923), who spent a small fortune improving the mansion house. He stocked it with paintings by a variety of British and continental artists. One particular country scene was an example of the work of Charles Jacque, who had been one of his intimate friends.

In 1408 Kendals was owned by the Duke of Exeter, son of John of Gaunt. From then until 1608 it was associated with royalty. James the First granted it to Robert Cecil, Earl of Salisbury, whose family held it until 1739 when it was bought and rebuilt by William Jephson, a rich wine merchant.

Jephson's niece married Robert Phillimore. It remained in the Phillimore family until 1889 under the title of Kendals Hall.

William Robert Phillimore took over Newberries and renamed it Organ Hall. He also added the manor house at Battlers Green to the Kendals estate.

The last of the direct Phillimore line (W.B. Phillimore) fought in the Crimean War as a captain in the 6th Dragoon Guards. It was he who gave the land for the building of Radlett Church. His wife had been Elizabeth Jane Sheldrake but died without issue in 1887. The property then went to his third cousin, Sir Walter Phillimore. He became Lord Phillimore, with a family seat at Henley, and bestowed Kendals on his eldest son R.C. Phillimore, a representative of the L.C.C. for Deptford. Some time before the Great War he set up a scheme for training east London girls in horticultural work at Battlers Green. He also built a block of flats near Srubbits and presented them to the poor of Radlett. He died in 1919 after having served in France during the war. His widow Lucy, nee Fitzpatrick, presented the Phillimore Recreational Ground to Radlett as a memorial to her husband in 1921. Discoveries made at the site of the Battlers Green property recently went on show at Watford Museum. Kendals has now become The Kendal Hall Country Club.

Aldenham house had been previously known as Wigbournes. Throughout its long history it had been associated with another mansion nearby known as Penns Place. Penns, as it was familiarly called, was sited near the Battleaxe public house, but was demolished in the 19th century. A family named Cade held it in the early part of the 14th century. In 1485 Sir Humphrey Coningsby bought it together with Wigbournes. Sir Humphry considered Radlett to be a rather pagan place at that time and constructed a small church on Cobden Hill, which became known as Chantry Chapel. The site is occupied today by a small cottage. Penns Place was acquired by the Coghill family in 1640.

Wigbournes had been founded by John Wykebourne in 1355 and was occupied sometime afterwards by one Robert West. He was succeeded by William Seres, noted for his work on the Cathedral Psalter and the 1549 Bible. By 1590 Thomas Sutton had acquired the property. Thomas had a daughter named Faith who married Henry Coghill, so uniting the two families. Penns was renamed Aldenham Hall, and Wigbournes was called Aldenham House.

Faith and Henry had a daughter who married Sir Christopher Wren, and it is thought that the latter lent some of his architectural skill when the mansion was reconstructed about that time.

Aldenham House passed eventually to Anthony Gibbs, later to become Lord Aldenham. He preferred to live at his other house, Clifton Hamden, in Oxfordshire. His brother, the Hon. Vicary Gibbs, and sister, Edith Gibbs, resided at Aldenham House from the late 19th to well into the 20th century. They were jointly responsible for the very high standard of beauty that the place achieved during that time.

Lord Aldenham and the Hon. Vicary Gibbs died within a short period of each other. Subsequent death duties caused the breaking up and selling of the estate. The house and grounds were acquired by the Haberdashery Company to form a teaching unit named

Haberdashers Aske School.

Radlett is fortunate in having two such well preserved links with her past as Kendals and Aldenham House. I well recall the latter as it used to be in the halcyon days of 70 years ago when, on

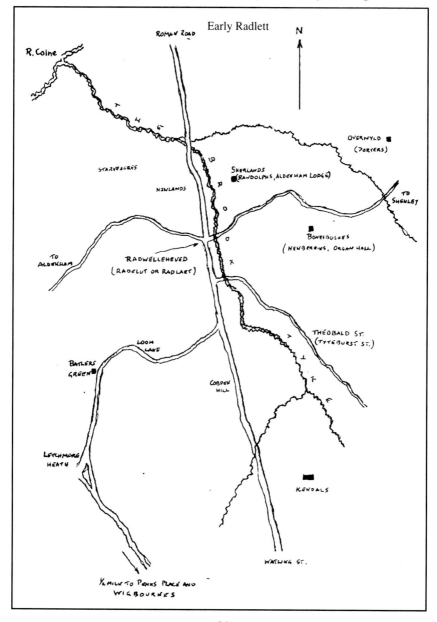

Early Radlett

Open Days, we were allowed to wander at will through its spacious grounds and beautiful gardens. We marvelled at the wide range of exotic plants gleaned, I understand, from many parts of Europe and America; some of them introduced into England for the first time. They were nurtured and tended in their new habitat by Mr Becket, the head gardener and his co-workers.

In late summer a Flower Show was usually arranged, people coming from miles around to view the wonderful floral displays that went on show each year.

EXTRACTS FROM THE BRITISH DICTIONARY
OF ARCHITECTS 1600-1840

Francis Wigg the First (1791-1868) was a member of the firm, originally Wigg and Mansfield, subsequently Wigg, Mansfield and Wigg; and eventually Wigg and Pownall, Builders, Surveyors and Architects. They had premises first at 10 North Place, Gray's Inn Lane; later at 7 Bedford Row. Francis Wigg and George Pownall exhibited plans at the Royal Academy in competition for the design of the Royal Exchange and the Liverpool Assize Court. They were employed by the Society of Gray's Inn, Holborn, for whom they designed the Italianate Library of 1841 (gutted by bombs in 1941) also the Jacobean Staples Inn Buildings 1842-43 (severely damaged in 1941). Another of their designs was the lodge and gates between the Staple Inn and Southampton Buildings. The firm continued after Elizabeth Wigg married into the Oliver family, under the name of Wigg, Son and Oliver, subsequently Wigg, Oliver and Hudson, until the end of the last century, while still at the 7 Bedford Row address.

Francis Wigg was the son of Joseph Wigg (1752-1824) who was a Surveyor to the Inner Temple and Master of the Tylers and Bricklayers Company in 1819-20. He owned considerable property in Hertfordshire including a large country house known as Frogmore Hall in the Parish of Aston.

The Small Proprietors

In addition to those large estates already mentioned, many of which had become veiled in the mists of time, a few smaller properties had been acquired in and around Park Street, Frogmore and Bricket Wood by the ordinary folk of the district, as far back as the early 17th century. On the 30th April, 1690, Robert Skeale, a bricklayer in the Parish of St. Stephen, made a will bequeathing five items of land and property lying around this area.

Item 1: Bequeathed to his wife Sarah. His messuage or tenement in which he lived, abutting on Smug Oak Green, Bricket Wood, together with 3 acres of land and all <u>houses, edifices</u>, <u>buildings</u>, <u>stables</u>, <u>gardens</u> and orchards (the underlined repeats itself after each of the other four items and will be denoted by 'etc.').

Item 2: Bequeathed to his grandson John Hawtree, son of his daughter Mary. His messuage or tenement, etc. known as Hartychoke in the Parish of St. Stephen, now occupied by John Gardner, and formerly by William Harting.

Item 3: Bequeathed to his granddaughter Sarah Hawtree. His messuage or tenement, etc. lying in Frogmore in the Parish of St. Stephen, now occupied by Rebecca Anderson.

Item 4: Bequeathed to his granddaughter Susan Hawtree. His messuage or tenement, etc. lying in Park Street, now occupied by Joseph Taylor.

Item 5: Bequeathed to his granddaughter Elizabeth Hawtree. His messuage or tenement, etc. lying and being on Bricket Wood, now occupied by Henry Carter.

The unabridged version of this will can be found in the book entitled *All My Worldly Goods* published by the Bricket Wood History Society.

      The three attractive gable-fronted cottages on Park Street

Lane just past the Fairhaven flats were once a block of five owned by the Anderson family, and were probably built by them. Members of the family were builders, stonemasons and carpenters in the village for several generations. In those days the cottages were numbered from 5 to 9, number 5 being a stonemason's and number 6 a carpenter's shop. In 1851 Benjamin Anderson and his wife Ann occupied number 7.

All five of the cottages were freehold, each having a front garden, a shed, and a garden at the back. The end wall of number 9 backed on to three ancient cottages, with one room up and one down, which were tithed to the workers of Park Valley Farm. A tall brick wall in the north shielded the property from one of the Park Valley Farm fields, while a shorter wall in the east separated them from a cottage belonging, at that time, to a Mistress Form.

On July 15th, 1851, Benjamin and his wife made an agreement with Joseph Anderson which allowed him to purchase numbers 5, 6 and 7. Numbers 8 and 9 were occupied, at that time, by J.W.J. Shaw and Joseph Andrews.

Will Martin (born 1796) purchased all five of the cottages in 1860 and in 1861 made a will leaving them to his wife Hannah. Hannah Martin died in 1866. In 1867 the cottages were occupied as follows:

No. 5 -   Joseph Andrews at £5 per annum
No. 6 -   Susan Linney at 1/9d weekly
No. 7 -   George Linney at 1/9d weekly
No. 8 -   Elizabeth Sharp at 1/9d weekly
No. 9 -   Joseph Worrell at 1/9d weekly.

Annual expenses: Poor and Highway Rates	£0.18. 9
Repairs for 1866	£1.12. 2
The Inland Revenue rateable was	£23. 4. 0.

On March 31st, 1903, an Indenture was made concerning the cottages worded as follows: *'Whereas Will Martin testator, blacksmith and common brewer, made a will dated 19.11.1861, leaving five freehold cottages to his wife Hannah for life, hence to trustees, sons George and John and son-in-law George Fenn, who should pay rent to his daughter Mary Edmunds, to divide between her heirs free from husband's control or in limitation of heirs 21 or over, the property to pass in fee simple to his own right heirs.'*

George Martin, one of the trustees, died in 1862 before the will could be executed. In September 1863 the will was proved by the surviving trustees, John Martin and George Fenn, in the solicitors' office of Sedgewick, Turner, Oddie and Swordee, Watford Place, on signature of Edmond G. Oddie.

In probate, John Martin and George Fenn attested that Mary Edmunds, born 10th August, 1826, was of the linear line of Will Martin. Hannah Martin died on the 26th of April, 1866, and Mary Edmunds, her daughter, on November 18th, 1902, leaving three children, Mary Ann Edmunds, Hannah Mariott and Catherine Edmunds (Catherine subsequently married Fred Martin); they each inherited a third share of the property. Later, Mary Ann, who had remained a spinster, purchased her sister Catherine's share. She was known to the family as Polly and just before she died she made a will bequeathing her two-thirds share to her sister Hannah Mariott, hence to her two nephews Walter and Arthur Marriott equally. To her sister Catherine Martin she left a gold watch and her house 'Mafeking' in Leavesden Road, Watford, which was subsequently left to her children Richard John, Ernest Edmund and Dorothy Charlotte Martin equally. The witnesses were Millicent Bowman Meikle and Lucy Wakeling.

CHAPTER 9
DOCUMENTS CONCERNING THE WIGG FAMILY MENTIONING PROPERTY ON THE PARK VALLEY ESTATE

1)   Abstract: Title to Lot 13 Frogmore Estate (1919) page 9, Bridgemen and Company, 4, College Hill, Cannon Street, London. (Citing Francis Wigg's will, 1864.) 1st December, 1864: Frogmore House and garden is described as 'that messuage and garden at Frogmore, the wash-house and the plantation in front, the meadow behind, in his own occupation; two cottages adjoining the wash-house, occupied by the families Anthony and Janes and the gardens of said cottage occupied by himself; and another two cottages [Drennan in my time] then occupied by George, but formerly occupied by Bisney [probably when they belonged to Cooper] and all those messuages or tenements, farmlands, woodlands and heriditaments being in occupation by George Beament and Charles Anderson or their undertenants'. [Note: Charles Anderson died 1875 - see *The Book of Park Street & Frogmore* p.57.]

Also two freehold fields called Hither Park Valley and Upper Park Valley, containing 15 acres and 9 perches in his own occupation, together with five cottages (south of Drennans) occupied by Smith, Toms, Bradshaw, Sharp and Harris, purchased by his late father (Joseph Wigg) from John Cooper.

Also to Francis 2nd, Carr and George Wigg and brother-in-law Joseph Sherwood, the schoolroom and matron-house and stables adjoining, to hold in trust for his daughter Elizabeth Ann Oliver and children.

Also the freehold dwelling-house, stable, garden-lands and previous tithe houses and appurtenances in the tenancy or occupation of W.H.E. Duncan (Spooners) and all the estate in the same parish (Little

Burston) purchased of William Costin, consisting of stable, garden and outhouses then in the occupation of Henry Costin, and two meadows and cattle shed in William Costin's own occupation and his cottages and lands in Park Street Lane occupied by Clark: also cottages and lands in Hyde Lane (purchased from Mead) together with the Pesthouse field and Kill Sow meadow in occupation of Henry Costin and his under-tenants, and the two cottages near the Pesthouse field in occupation by Fen and Elwood and those cottages in Park Street Lane and in Bury Dell in occupation of Dayton, Simmons, Stocksley, Smith, Boff and Deyton.

Two cottages in occupation by William Dickinson and Eason and two in occupation by Benjamin Dickinson and Trapp [note there was a Joseph Dickinson, tenant farmer, at Burston in 1878] and his messuage and garden purchased from Mrs Henley's trustees and leased to William Maskell Harvey all freehold or copyhold. Also to the aforementioned Francis and Carr and brother George Wigg, and brother-in-law Joseph Sherwood, all those old and new shares in Chelsea Water Works and certain freehold and leasehold properties in the County of Middlesex and Surrey. [A proviso adds that Francis 1st's widow should continue as tenant of the two cottages next to the wash-house for £80 per annum, providing that she did not remarry.]

2)   26th February, 1868, the above testator, Francis Wigg died. His will was proved in the Principal Registry of Court of Probate, by the executors mentioned and sworn under assuity of £60,000 (stamp duties £600 and £150).

In 1867, previous to the death of the testator, three pieces of land containing 1 rood and 16 perches, 1 acre and 13 perches, and 1 acre, 3 roods and 64 perches were taken for the purpose of a line for the Midland Railway: total £950.

7th April, 1873, by Deed Poll made by the previously

70

mentioned inheritors of the property acting with the Revd. Marcus Richard Southwell and the Revd. Frederick Lipscombe, grant and convey the schoolroom and premises to hold as tenants-in-common for use as a school.

February 24th, 1886. A piece of land 1 acre 26 perches, lying in Common Mead near Bricket Wood (number 810 on the Ordinance map) a part of the aforementioned inheritance, was conveyed to A.H.H. Hibbert for £35.

July 1st, 1889. Francis 2nd died leaving his wife Caroline Maria with no powers under the will in her favour. As certain portions of the copyhold property had been, from time to time, enfranchised by F. and C. Wigg at their own expense, an Indenture was made on May 1st, 1890 between Carr Wigg, 11 Queen Victoria Street, and his wife Alice Louisa Nona Wigg; Harry Oliver of 5, Queens Gardens, Hyde Park, and his wife Elizabeth Ann; the Revd. Henry Francis Oliver of Brancote, Stevenage, Andrew Oliver of 5, Queens Gardens, Mary Elizabeth and Katherine Janet Oliver, spinsters, and John Russell Thomson Robertson of 11, Queen Victoria Street, as inheritors; and Henry Trelawney Boodle (first part), the Right Hon. Arthur Algernon, Earl of Essex (second part), and F. and C. Wigg (third part) as trustees. The copyhold property, duly enfranchised, included cottages occupied by Fenn and Elwood; Pesthouse field; cottages on land in Hyde Lane (purchased by Mead), the buildings having been pulled down by C. Wigg and the sites made part of the Pesthouse field; also other cottages in Berry Dell, pulled down and rebuilt at his own expense; also cottages once occupied by Benjamin Dickinson and Eason. The three almshouses erected on the site were handed over in trust to the two vicars of St. Stephens and Holy Trinity.

March 10th, 1891. The surviving Wigg and Oliver families and John Oddie and Ilted Nichol, by virtue of the Land Transfer Act, conveyed a piece of land of about two roods, forming a

71

part of Upper Park Valley field [in occupation, at that time, by S. Brunton] for the purpose of and use as a burial ground (freely and voluntarily).

October 29th, 1895. At the office of Messrs. Bridgman and Company, 4, College Hill, Cannon Street, London: Indenture between A. Oliver (mortgagor) first, Carr Wigg second, and the Revd. Francis Oliver of the Vicarage, Scawby, Lincolnshire (mortgagee). Agreement for a share loan of £2,000. Covenant for payment of principal and interest. Mortgagor as beneficial owner conveys to mortgagee income from remaining heriditaments. Redemption and reconveyance on payment of money advanced.

Schedule of Property, 1895

House and carpenter's shop, outbuildings, garden and builder's yard; let to Mrs.Rentowl. Two cottages in occupation by Humbles and Smith, four modern adjacent cottages in occupation by Gurney, Norwood, Ewer, and Dickinson (fronting main road, with gardens); Ver Cottage, Park Valley Farm, 195 acres, let to Thomas Mead; piece of land at end of Branch Road, 19 perches, let to Thomas Mead; Buttercup Meadow in Berry Dell Lane, 3 acres, 34 perches, let to William Chaffy Giddens. Grass and arable field adjoining Holy Trinity known as Upper Park Valley, five and one-half acres, let to S. Brunton; house, with outbuildings and garden opposite Holy Trinity Church, let to Henry Costin and occupied by Jefferies. Two cottages next to Alms Houses in occupation by Ashby and Trapp. Five cottages in Berry Dell Lane, occupied by Eames, Garrett, Cook, Smith and Martin. Residence known as Park Cottage with garden, paddocks, stables and outbuilding, 1 acre, 1 rood, 13 perches, let to Thomas Gowland Page. Two cottages and gardens (Homestead), 3 roods, 30 perches, let to Harding. Residence known as Spooners with gardens, paddocks, pleasure grounds, stables and coach house, 5 acres, 2 roods, 22 perches, let to

Miss Winter. Two arable and one grass field (previously Kill Sow and Pesthouse meadows) 19 acres, 3 roods, 5 perches, let to Henry Costin [part subsequently became a golf course]. Stroud Wood, 12 acres, 1 rood [went to the making of H.P. aerodrome], two meadows and part of James George's garden opposite Holy Trinity Church, 7 acres, then in hands of James George's executors [became 'Roundabouts' grazing area], house and grounds known as St. Stephens Cottage, occupied by Miss Lewis. An Indenture executed by Andrew Oliver and Henry F. Oliver concerning estate income, made by Alice Louisa Nona Wigg of The Gables, 16 The Drive, Hove, Sussex, and the Revd. Francis Oliver, The Vicarage, Fenny Stratford, Bucks., on the one part, and Andrew, Mary and Katherine Oliver as beneficiaries.

'All real estate heridits and premes situated in the said parish, together with rents and profits, might merge and be extinguished in the equitable reversion and inheritance thereof and that the beneficiaries might become entitled to the said premes for an equitable estate in fee simple in possession.'

Schedule of Inherits and Premes
Part 1.

Freehold detached residence Park Street Lodge (Spooners) let to Henrietta Esther Elwes, 1908, on a three-year tenancy [Walker took over in 1909 and was followed a few years later by Eldred] at £80 a year. Two freehold, one grass and one arable field situated in Hyde Lane, 19 acres, 3 roods, 5 perches, let to S. Brunton as yearly tenant at £25 per year. Brick and tiled cottage known as Church Cottage with garden and timber-built stable and cart shed, let to Mrs. Ellen Costin at £15 p.a. plus rates and taxes.

Park Cottage, outbuildings, etc. 1 acre, 1 rood, 13 perches, let to Thomas Page at £30 p.a. Two run-down brick and timber cottages (orchard) four rooms in each, let to Cleaver and Widow Shephard at 2/-

each, landlord paying rates and taxes. Two brick and timber cottages Jacobs, one having two rooms up and two down, and the other three up and three down with garden, orchard and timber-built stable and cart shed, 3 roods, 30 perches, let to Charles Kirby at 25/- per month plus rates and taxes.

Burydell cottages, total rent 13/2d with landlord paying rates and taxes, occupied by Eames, Garrett, Worker, Smith and Martin (1908). Two brick and tiled cottages near to new Alms Houses, five rooms with garden at rear, let to Dickinson and Trapp; joint rent 5/2d per week, minus rates and taxes. Two meadows opposite Holy Trinity Church known as 'Round' and 'Roundabout', total 6 acres, 1 rood, 10 perches with three enclosed cattle sheds in occupation of Henry George at £17 p.a. minus [minus = landlord pays rates and taxes]. Old-fashioned freehold brick-built and tiled cottage with small grounds near St. Stephens Church, known as St. Stephens Cottage. Let on a repairing lease to Simon Henry Leeder at £60 p.a.

Part 2.

No. 84 Park Street, let to Mrs. Rentowl at £20 p.a. plus rates, etc. Sam Lee's cottage and first school at rear let to Mrs. Lee and Mrs. Lauman; rent, the two together, 6/- per week minus. Four brick-built and tiled cottages fronting the main road with gardens, let to Gurney, Dickinson, Evans and Ewer; total rent 13/4d minus. A freehold farm, known as Park Valley Farm containing 195 acres with a house, two cottages and two homesteads, let to Sidney Brunton at £197.10.0 p.a., tenant doing repairs and landlord finding materials. A freehold meadow in Berry Dell Lane 3 acres, 34 perches, let to W. Chaffy Giddens at £10 p.a. (known as Buttercup Meadow with ditch running through lined with trees). Ver Cottage, with 2 reception, 4 bed, 1 bath, kitchen, scullery, W.C., woodhouse, greenhouse, and garden. Let to Miss Marion Ferguson at £35 p.a. 26th April, 1904. Indenture between Trustees and Beneficiaries. F. Wigg purchased part of meadow (22 perches) called

Road Meadow from William Costin, being a part of a garden and premises owned by Carr Wigg (transfer of part of willed land from Oliver to Wigg) citing will of F. Wigg, 13th July, 1899, *'...piece of land with abuttals, as drawn on plan, together with right of way; to be used as school for poor persons in the two parishes St. Stephens and Frogmore'.*

N.B. Leasehold property in London is not the subject of these extracts Indenture, 29th November, 1909. Between mortgagor Henry Francis Oliver and the mortgagees John Mackenzie Hanbury, The Brewery, Spitalfields; Arthur Dighton Annesley of Burns Close, Amberley, Gloucestershire, and Francis Cotton Ambersley of 35, Lincoln's Inn Fields. In consideration of £1,500 paid to mortgagor a quarter share of aforementioned estate and interest accruing goes to mortgagee.

Schedule of Conveyance

A. The Park Street Lodge let to Nigel O. Walker on a thirteen-year lease from 24th June, 1909 at £80 p.a.

B. Two arable and one grass fields in Hyde Lane, 19 acres, 5 roods, 5 perches; let to S. Brunton at £25 p.a. [site of golf links].

C. Church Cottage, let to Streather at 8/- per week.

D. Park Cottage, 1 acre, 1 rood, 13 perches, let to Page for twenty-one years from 1904 (determined after seven or fourteen years) at £30 p.a.

E. Orchard Cottage, let to Cleaver and Bonwick at 2/3d each p.w.

F. 'Jacobs', 3 roods, 30 perches, let to Muskett at £1. 6. 8 per month plus rates and taxes.

G. Berry Dell Cottages. Eames, Garrett, Ewett, Hornett, Martin, £45 p.a. total.

H. Two cottages next to new Alms Houses [was barber's, now residences] let to George and Dickinson, 5/9d total p.w.

I. Round and Roundabout meadows, 6 acres, 1 rood, 10 perches, let at an annual rent of £17.

J & K. Cottages Lee and Western (opposite 84) £15.12. 0. p.a. minus.

L. Four cottages with gardens facing main road, Gurney, Evans, Ewer, Dickinson, £34.13. 4 p.a.

M. Park Valley Farm 195 acres, £197.10. 0. p.a.

N. Meadow, five and one-half acres with path to Stroud Wood let to S. Brunton at £10 p.a.

O. Stroud Wood 12 acres, 1 rood.

P. Ver Cottage, let to Perkins at £35 p.a.

Q. Meadow (Buttercup) 3 acres, 34 perches, let to Stanley Giddens at £10 p.a.

R. A piece of land at end of Branch Road, let to S. Brunton.

On 31st June, 1912, J.H. Fischer declared the Revd. Henry Francis Oliver of unsound mind in the office of the Masters of Lunacy. He was replaced as executor by Ethel Marion Oliver of 2, Woodlands Road, Littlehampton (his wife) and Katherine Janet Oliver of 5, Queens Gardens, Hyde Park (spinster) as receivers of the Estate.

Christmas Day 1915: In his will of this date Henry Francis Oliver, M.A. of Brunswick Road, Kingston-on-Thames, Clerk in Holy Orders, appointed his sons Cyril F.H. Oliver and Theodore B. Oliver executors and trustees of his will. He left all his property that he had power to dispose of to C.F.H. Oliver and T.B. Oliver with all powers of sale and conversion, authorising them to postpone sale for as long as they might think fit. The will was signed by the Testator and duly attested by A.G. Davison, steward, 8, Brunswick Road, Kingston-on-Thames, and A.E. Davison, ironmonger, 5, The Broadway, Crowborough, Sussex. C.F.H. Oliver died in 1916 without having proved the will.

September 11th, 1919: Conveyance between Andrew, Mary Elizabeth, Katherine Janet and Theodore Bernard, Oliver and James John Pinnock. One piece of land known as Berrydell Meadow fronting Berrydell Lane by 83 yards, comprising 3 acres, 35 poles. Secondly, piece of land conveyed on December 2nd, 1915 between William Sharp and Arthur William Tansley and Evelyn Mary Dove to keep a portion of the river marked A and B in good condition for the working of the mill (referred to as Corville). Thirdly, parcel of land, formerly part of Park Valley Farm (Ord. No. 38), with an area of 0.315 acres; identified on a conveyance, 8th November, 1950, between William John Honour and James John Pinnock.

The Boff Territory:

F. Wigg, the 2nd, by will dated 24th April, 1883, bequeathed several parts of his property to be sold by A. Banks, 11, Gray's Inn Place, Gray's Inn Road, and John Owen of 27, Cornhill, London. That piece of land, in area 1514 ft., formerly part of meadow on estate of Thomas Kinder forming a part of garden of cottage formerly occupied by John William Woodstock, now by George Boff, abutting towards the east on the other part of said garden, on New Branch Road to the north, on a meadow adjoining to the west, and in the south, the said cottage. Also a piece of meadow ground 1 rood, 22 perches formerly belonging to White Horse Estate also the property of Thomas Kinder and in occupation of G. Boff, with right of passage for horses, carts and cattle along the New Branch Road held from the Lord of the Manor by a yearly rent of 1d. Also four poles with cottage thereon, lately occupied by Mrs. Bates, then by Zachariah Barr, then by John W. Woodstock and finally, by George Boff. Held previously to 11th April, 1878 by Lord of the Manor, yearly rent 6d.

July 7th, 1906: Marion Jane Boff, widow of Henry Boff, who died intestate, conveyed his share to George Boff for an annuity of £72 providing whole estate was charged with payment of annuity on death of George (batchelor). Schedule of Boff property at that time: Nos. 17 and 31 Sopwell Lane, the Red Cow, Colney Street. Dwelling house occupied by George Boff and all outbuildings on the site plus two cottages adjoining dwelling house. Nine cottages and the freehold villas forming Lots 18, 19, 21, 22, and 95 of Radlett Building Estate. Also pieces of land Lots 16, 17, 18, 21, 22, 95, 128, 129, 130, 131, of the said estate, heriditaments bought by George and Harry Boff for £920 on 5th March, 1890. [In February 1886 G. and H. Boff claimed as treasure trove 221 coins found in their timber yard.]

George Boff died on 6th April, 1907. In June, 1908, Marcus Boff of 36, St. Albans Road, Watford, representing Marion Jane Boff of Park Street by virtue of the Land Transfer Act 1897, released to Arthur Tremayne Buller of 12, Ridgemont Road, St. Albans, for the sum of £305, the two cottages known as 140 and 141 Park Street in occupation, at that time, by Ellen Ann Goodman and James Sheppard, providing an annuity of £72 be made to Jane Boff.

July 1st, 1919: The widow of Arthur Tremayne Buller, now living in Devon, sold the two freehold cottages, then occupied by Mrs. Goodman and George Sweby, for a net sum of £270, after certain property liabilities had been met, to Ethel Louisa Taylor, wife of Leonard Alfred Page Taylor of Moor Mill.

June 15th, 1953: Ethel Taylor, now widowed, sold to Ronald Bragg one of the freehold cottages now known as 90 Park Street, to be used as office and living quarters. In 1959 Ronald Bragg bought the other cottage known as 92 Park Street from Vienne Marie Cunningham, then living at Flat 5, Knollys House, Tavistock Place, London, for the sum of £800.

[Note: The Boff dwelling house had been occupied by Mr Hayter since the film development company Lillywhites vacated the premises (see page 92 of *An Edwardian Village and its People*).]

Frogmore House, the Wiggs' country mansion, built in 1819. Author Cyril Martin is seen standing in what was left of the once beautiful front garden. (1981)

CHAPTER 10

HISTORY OF BURSTON MANOR

About the year 50 B.C. a track was made through the dense forest at Burston by some Iron Age people known as the Belgae. The track connected their oppidum at Prae Wood with the head waters of the River Ver at Frogmore where they had made a small settlement. Several clearings along the track were cultivated.

When the Romans arrived in this district about A.D. 43 they took over the patches of cultivation and the wattle and daub buildings of the Belgae and built some of their own. They built a really impressive stone villa on the Iron Age people's settlement near the river (both discovered and excavated in 1943). From then onwards Burston became a very important district.

In the year 793 A.D. the Saxon King Offa of Mercia founded a monastery in honour of St. Alban the first British Christian martyr and put an abbot in charge of it. Records were kept by the scribes of the monastery of all the land around the district.

In the year 1225 a record was made of an addition of one hide being added to Burston by Robert Fitz-Hame. In 1300 it was held leasehold by a Roger de Brok, while a John de Charleton held the freehold. In 1333 a life interest was given to William de Brok, son of Roger, with reversion after his death to John de Charleton who proposed dividing it between his own son, John Charleton, his wife Matilda, and John de Triple of London. It was reported that William de Brok, in an imbecilic fit of rage, attempted to kill young John Charleton but was restrained by John Golape, a groom, who tied him to a tree until he had cooled down.

In 1348 the said John, son of John de Charleton, released to William all claims to Burston Manor. About 1400, Abbot Heyworth purchased the estate and reinstalled the Charleton family. In 1436 Sir

Thomas Charleton and his wife Elizabeth conveyed the manor to John Fry and his wife Alice. Fry at that time was Baron of the Exchequer. The estate was valued as follows:

263 acres of arable land at 4d. an acre

56 acres of pasture land at 3d. an acre

8 acres of meadow land at 12d. an acre.

In 1438 Henry VI (1421-1471) granted a licence to John of Wheathampstead (Abbot of St. Albans 1420-1440) to purchase Burston Manor from John Fry. It was held by the monastery until 1480. From 1480 until 1518 it was under lease to John Kyng and indentured to Rojer Roysse for 31 years. Twenty years later it demised to Ralph Rowlatt for a further 40 years. After the Dissolution Burston came to the King, who gave it to Anthony Denny Esq. with Nicholas Bacon as trustee. He granted it to Thomas Skepworth in 1556 at a rent of one-tenth of a knight's fee £1. 0.10. Skepworth leased the whole manor to Martin Veale for the use of Dorothy Maynarde, widow, for life. After her second marriage she conveyed it to her husband Francis Rojers (his family had once held the estate of Meridon {Munden}).

In 1556 the King gave a licence to alienate the manor. It came into the hands of a family named Kentish. In 1642 William Kentish settled it on his wife, Rose, who was the daughter of Robert Nichol. William Kentish's son, also named William, willed the manor to his two daughters Sarah, wife of Godman Jenkins, and Mary, wife of Thomas Nichol. In 1746 Godman Jenkins was in sole possession and, when he died, he left the property to his daughter, Sarah, who had married twice, once to M. Newdigate and then to Samuel Nichol. She outlived them both and died in 1767, still in possession of the manor, which then passed to another Sarah, wife of Robert Hucks of Aldenham.

Sarah Hucks died in 1771(?) and left the property to her son Robert Hucks. He died, unmarried, in 1814 and the estate descended to two nieces, Sarah and Ann Noyes. They both died in 1841. Following their death, Burston came to Henry Hucks, Baron Aldenham, then living at St. Dunstans, Regents Park, London.

After Henry Hucks death in 1907, the Right Honourable Alban George Henry Gibbs inherited both title and property, sharing the copyhold part set out in Schedule 2 with Antony Gibbs at Tynksfield, Somerset, and George Edward Cokyne, the late Baron's cousin and brother-in-law who were also trustees and executors of the will.

THE BURSTON ESTATE 1910

Schedule 1

Tenants 1913		A R P
Archibald Muir, Manor Farmand	Land, house, cottages barns, etc.	226 0 27
Tom Smith, Darley Hall	Manor farmland and cottages	144 3 1
John Thrale, Slowmans	Woods and cottage	<u>67 1 21</u>
		<u>438 3 9</u>

Schedule 2

	A R P
Copyhold to the Manor of Park	
Part of Burston Woods	15 2 33
Part of Manor Farm	8 3 11
Part of Lodge	<u>128 3 3</u>
	<u>153 1 7</u>

Schedule 3

Freehold Land (occupied by			
Henry Costin)	58	3	33
Sold to Francis Wigg Esq. (enfranchised	5	0	39
in 1914) then sold to Lt. Col. Bigge			
and R. Harrison	4	3	20
Previously conveyed to L. and N.W.	4	0	1
Railway Co.			
	1	0	20
	9	0	37
	11	2	27
	7	0	20

In March 1914 Baron Aldenham and trustees paid £690.5.6 to the Rt. Hon. George Devereaux de Vere, Earl of Essex (Lord of the Manor of Park) for the Burston heriditaments to be enfranchised.

In September 1920 all the property set out in Schedules 1 and 2, except the Tippingdell Lodge premises, was conveyed to Reginald Foster of Lye House, Bricket Wood, Director of Public Companies, for £14,000. The following Terrier describes the names and size of the fields.

Part 1

	A	R	P
The Shaw (cartway)	0	3	21
Almond Field	11	0	25
How Wood Field	9	3	25
Horse-pond Mead	3	2	31
Birch Wood	4	3	10
Middle Mead	3	1	5
Cowleys Wood	14	0	21
Little Brick Miln Field	3	2	31
Young Wood	2	3	9
Lower Mead	4	3	0
Round Wood	4	3	7
Four Acres	4	0	22
Furze Wood	3	1	16
Further Cow Pasture	9	3	8
Hanestead and Garden	1	2	27
Hither Cow Pasture	8	2	23
Great Orchard	7	2	5
Orchard Field	6	0	38
Hoppitt (cartway)	0	3	22
Pond Field	3	1	5
Little Orchard	1	2	36
Sixteen Acres	13	1	31
Hither Fore Field	8	1	35
Tippendales	8	2	6
Footpath Fore Field	8	2	37
Little How Field	10	1	29
Further Sprawleys	14	3	26
Great How Field	21	3	9
Middle Sprawleys	16	1	28
Further Clay Pit Field	8	3	19
Hither Sprawley	11	3	36
Broom Field	4	1	33
Burston Broom	6	2	29
Common Mead Piece	0	1	13
Great Brick Kiln Field	18	1	34
Total Acreage	274	2	32

Part 2

	A	R	P
House, yard and garden	1	0	28
Home Mead	1	1	7
Part of Garden Field	5	0	13
Six Acres	1	3	14
Part of Six Acres	3	2	20
Part of Garden Field)			
Rush Mead)	6	0	4
Well Spring)			
Two Acres	2	1	10
Part of Round Wood	4	2	32
Plantation	0	3	0
Poor Field	6	2	11
Poor Field	3	0	21
Four Acrea)			
Borrowsons Field)	17	0	36
Longs Field)			
Linneys Spring	10	3	10
Cross Path Field	13	3	37
Slowman Field	10	0	34
Orchard and two cottages	2	2	3
Further Smugs (?)			
Hither Smugs	9	2	32
Arable field plus small wood	8	3	29
Total Acreage	109	3	21
	==========		

Part 3

	A	R	P
Nine Acrea	9	2	18
Meadow	4	0	5
Darley Hall Meadow	4	2	31
Meadow	0	0	18
Little Meadow	1	3	20
Upper Grounds	38	2	21
Total Aceeage	58	3	33
Total Area	443	2	6

Executed and attested by Lord Aldenham,   H. C. Gibbs & G. H. B. Gibbs

85

Shortly after purchasing the Burston property R. Foster obtained a loan of £9,500 at 6% from Baron Aldenham and the trustees of the estate, mortgaging the estate as security.

On 12th April, 1923 an Indenture was made between the Baron and trustees as mortgagees (1st part), C.W.B. Lock, Estate Agent of Station Road, Watford (3rd part), and Walter and Dudley Wilkins, builders (4th part), as purchasers. It was witnessed that in consequence of the sum of £8,960 paid by purchasers by direction of the vendor, the said C.W.B. Lock thereby conveyed and confirmed unto the purchasers all the "property" described in the Conveyance dated September 24, 1920; with the exception of the premises known as Tippingdell Lodge.

```
BURSTON MANOR FARM (present nomenclature)
                               A    R    P
Arable                         42   3    38
Arable and gravel pit          18   1    30
Grass                          44   3    33
Orchard                         7   1    32
Orchard                        14   2    11
Arable                         28   3    11
Pasture                        25   0    16
Pasture                         4   0    12
Arable                         21   3     0
Pasture                        10   0    18
House and buildings             1  32     2
Pond                            0   0    27
Moat                            0   0    27
Road                            0   3     5
Burston cottages                0   0    39
Keeper's cottage                0   1     0
                              221   2     1
```

	A	R	P
Grass	9	1	35
Cottage (Slowmans)	0	0	19
Arable	34	2	25
Arable	12	2	15
Ness cottages	2	2	9
Pasture	8	3	26
	68	3	9

WOODLAND

	A	R	P
How Wood	19	3	27
Birch Wood	8	1	21
Cowleys Wood	14	0	21
Wood	0	3	21
The Plantation	6	3	22
No name	3	0	28
Round Wood	12	2	20
No name	0	2	35
No name	0	2	13
	67	1	8

| TOTAL AREA | 357 | 2 | 18 |

Prior to the auction of the whole of Burston Estate, which had been divided into 46 Lots for disposal at the Peahen Hotel, St. Albans, one section, comprising the Manor House, three cottages, eighty-one acres of woods and open fields, was conveyed to Major George Harrison Townson of Leinster Court, Hyde Park, London, for the sum of £3,900. Two of the cottages mentioned in the conveyance, occupied by the families King and Twin, were situated near the exit of the drive from the Manor House into the Watford road. The other cottage, standing at the north-east corner of Birchwood was originally a keeper's cottage, built in old style flint and timber. At the time of the sale it was in use as a cattery. The conveyance stated that the purchasers had to bear two-thirds of the cost of maintaining the drive to the Manor House; also he or she must erect a fence bordering field number 642. That territory, as well as a few others, were marked 'Sold' on the estate agent's map available at the auction.

The auction took place in June 1923, under the capable auspices of the estate agents Stimpson, Lock and Vince; after which most of the lots were successfully conveyed to the respective new owners.

On 21st August, 1923, lot 37 was conveyed to Lillian Kate Williams of 51a, Queens Road, Watford, for the sum of £1,050. That lot contained two old houses known as Ness cottages. Between lots 37 and 36 ran an ancient cartway into Burston. That cartway was brought up to residential standards and some of the frontage sold for building. Later, another road was constructed from Park Street Lane to follow the western boundary of lot 37 and join the new road near the cottage known as Slowmans; the whole of that loop road then became known as Burston Drive. Lot 36, on the north side of it, was also developed for housing and the old Slowmans cottage pulled down.

At the time of the sale most conveyances carried clauses stipulating that the land should be used for private housing, poultry farms or small holdings only, 'No dwelling house shall be erected without the plans having been submitted and approved by the vendors, who reserve the right to modify those conditions for any of the lots remaining unsold'. Lots 36 and 37 carried a further condition that the cartway to Burston Manor (albeit the new road) be fenced and maintained as a permanent right-of-way to the Manor House.

It would be interesting to know if the legal minds that thought up and promulgated those conditions were aware of the real antiquity of that cartway. It was the first man-made track through the forest in this area and in use long before the Romans came. One wonders also, could they have visualised the mushroom growth of roads, heavy traffic, houses and shops that would spring up as a result of the sale?

In March 1926, Major Townson conveyed his portion of the estate to Edwin Henry Bliss of 5, Raymond Buildings, Gray's Inn, London, for £4,000. Bliss disposed of fifteen acres of How Wood for building (in November 1937) to Kenneth Morrison Walters of 'Hilperton,' Mount Drive, Park Street, for £675.

The rest of Burston, the Manor House itself, the gardens, surrounding fields and woods, were sold on 19th September, 1962 by the estate agents, Mandley and Sparrow.

With that particular sale came the demise of one of Hertfordshire's very important estates, with which fate had dealt kindly for over two millenia.

CHAPTER 11
LYE HOUSE

The ill-drained, often flooded, winding course of Lye Lane was once a mere cart track to Blackgreen Cottage at the edge of a vast area of woodland. Sometime in the dim past a large country house had been built to the west of it a few hundred yards from its junction with the Watford road. The house stood in its own attractive grounds with   gardens, lawns and groups of trees, hardwoods and conifers. In 1862 Col. Thomas Edward Bigge came there to live. He was followed in 1886 by a hero of the Crimean and Indian wars, Major General Thomas Scovell Bigge, born 6th July, 1837. During the battle of Balaclava, while only eighteen years old, he suffered injury and was probably one of the casualties taken to the hospital at Scutari set up by Florence Nightingale. His wounds may have been dressed by 'The Lady of the Lamp' herself. He was mentioned in despatches and on reaching Sebastopol received two medals, a British medal and clasp, and one from the Turks called 'The Order of Medjidie'. After the Crimean war his military service took him to China and India, where he fought in the first and second Defence of Alumbagh as well as the campaign in Oude. Finally, he was decorated again with a medal and two clasps at the Relief and Capture of Lucknow.

In 1866 he married Ellen, a daughter of the Revd. and Lady Lees, the youngest daughter of the eleventh Earl of Huntingdon. They had three sons who were all educated privately. As Major General he became J.P. for Hertfordshire and lived at Lye House until his death on 14th May, 1914.

Reginald Foster took over Lye House from 1915 to 1922, but by 1923 John Percy Hall had moved in and stayed there until 1931. By that time a new house had been built on the opposite side of Lye Lane also named Lye House.

The old Lye House then stood unoccupied until, in 1932, after some structural alterations, it became a teaching centre named Tenterden Hall School (Proprietor, Frederick Smurthwaite, M.A.). In 1941 it was again vacated and ultimately became an annexe to Cell Barnes Hospital in 1949. By 1989 another change had taken place and it became Tenterden House Nursing Home.

The latest development has had the fields and groups of trees surrounding the house landscaped into an attractive golf links by the owner, John Pearson. A current development of the Lye House grounds is the building of an E.M.I. nursing unit between the existing nursing home and the proposed golf links.

THE NOKE AND THE HOLT PROPERTIES

Opposite the junction of Lye Lane and the Watford road, which was once a carriage turnpike track from Hatfield to Bath, is another small lane leading to two very ancient farms, The Noke and The Holt. The Noke farmhouse, together with a number of barns and two cottages, is situated a quarter of a mile down the lane and takes its name from them. This particular property was a part of the Burston Manor estate. In 1880 Baron Aldenham leased some of its land, known as Whips Heath, and a house, built on the Watford road in the early 19th century, to Mary Austin for the sum of £799. 5. 4. She obtained freehold a few years later.

On August 2nd, 1917, William Fisk, a St. Albans draper, bought Whips Heath and the Noke Farm, including machinery and growing crops, for the sum of £2,450 from Elsie Wallace Speers, wife of a local merchant. In 1919 William Fisk sold some of the property to Whitbread Priest Roberts.

When the house on the main road was subsequently converted into an hotel, mention was made in the deeds that the attractive oak panelling from the old house would be retained in the reception room of the new building. What is left of the old building is now just one small section of a complex hotel, The Noke Thistle Hotel, fully described as follows:

Four star hotel, the old house dating from the early nine teenth century and built of brick beneath hipped slate covered roofs. It is formed predominantly on two storeys, with a single storey modern extension to the front. A two storey bedroom extension was added about 20 years ago and is of concrete frame construction, with concrete cladding panels, beneath a flat roof. A further two storey bedroom extension was completed in the early part of 1990 and is of brick construction beneath a hipped slate covered roof. There are 111 bedrooms, including two suites, each with en-suite bathroom. Restaurant, cocktail bar, public bar and bistro, various conference and meeting rooms and a number of syndi cate rooms. There is car parking for 150 cars. Freehold.

Further information is extracted from a letter from Mr Russell Davidson, Partner at Dibb, Lupton, Broomhead, Solicitors:

The Abstracts of Title give the name of the Victorian owners, who appear to have included the Lord of the Manor of Burston. I remember noticing a Mary Austin room at the hotel when I visited it and I see that in 1854 a Mary Austin appears to have been tenant of the Manor and then to have purchased the property in 1880.

It appears that Mary Austin's interest in the property was copyhold - this was an ancient feudal way of holding land which was abolished under the Law of Property Act 1922. The copyhold owner was deemed to

hold the land as tenant of the Lord of the Manor and had
to get permission from the Lord of the Manor to sell his
or her interest to a new owner. By the eighteenth century
the Courts were holding that such permission could not,
in normal circumstances, be withheld, although the
tenant still had to turn up at the local manorial court,
which would give permission on behalf of the Lord of the
Manor for the sale to take place. It can be readily
appreciated that in time this formality became nothing
more than a nuisance, hence its abolition. The 1922 Act
made all copyhold land freehold and allowed the former
copyholder to buy out many of the Lord of the Manor's
rights.

In the case of the Noke Thistle, it looks as if Mary
Austin bought out the Lord of the Manor's rights in
advance of 1922, as after 1880 the property ceases to be
referred to as copyhold land and is pursuant to the
Copyhold Acts of 1852 and 1853 (there was another in
1887, consolidated in the Copyhold Act of 1894) which
enabled either Lord or tenant to secure compulsory
enfranchisement.

THE HOLT PROPERTY

A quarter of a mile further down Noke Lane another small road leads southwards to Holt farmhouse, a very spectacular residence which, together with its land, dates back to 1068 when it formed a part of the Manor of Windridge.

During the 14th century it became one of the important territories controlled by the Abbot of St. Albans. In 1368 the homestead was occupied by Joan Atte Holte, who was rebuked by the Abbot, at that time Thomas de la Mare, for failing to carry out repairs to the property. During the Wars of the Roses the farm and homestead were in possession of Sir Charles Fortesque. He had been supporting the Lancastrians and when the Yorkists gained the throne he had to forfeit the property to them. About one hundred years later St Thomas Seymour, who held the property at that time, not only had to lose possession of it but had to suffer the 'extreme penalty' at the same time.

In 1679 the Grimston family of Gorhambury took over the Holt property and held it until 1978, when a Dutchman Jo van de Putten and his wife Frances purchased the house and 360 acres of land. They have a town house in Jamert, Holland, near the Dutch-German border. Not long afterwards much of the Holt farmland was lost to the construction of the M25 and, in July 1981, the impressive homestead with its eleven bedrooms, five reception rooms, three bathrooms, offices, a granary, stables, two barns and ten acres of land, came on the market for £225,000.

THE HANSTEAD ESTATE

The history of Sir David and Lady Yule and their estate in Bricket Wood can be found in *The Book of Park Street and Frogmore*. A part of the demise of that estate with Agreements and maps dated February lst, 1921 are shown below.

Sir David is buried in the grounds of Hanstead Estate. The photograph above shows a view of his tomb and the magnificent ornamental iron-work surrounding it. The jacket shows a view of the splendid wrought-iron gate, designed and constructed by the local blacksmith, Herbert Martin, (the author's father). That gate is situated in the middle of the balustrade facing the front of Hanstead House.

An Agreement made the FIRST ——————day of FEBRUARY One thousand nine hundred and TWENTY ONE.

BETWEEN Sir DAVID YULE

of Hanstead House in the County of Hertford

(hereinafter called the "Landlord," which term shall include his Heirs, Executors, Administrators, and Assigns) of the one part, and LEONARD A. P. TAYLOR

of Moor Mills, Colney Street,

in the County of Hertford (hereinafter called

the "Tenant," which term shall include his Executors and Administrators) of the other part.

Description. IN CONSIDERATION of the rents, covenants, and agreements hereinafter reserved

any previous notice, to re-enter upon the lands and premises and to expel and put out the Tenant and all others therefrom, without prejudice to any other remedy, claim, or demand of the Landlords in respect of the same, or any other breach of this agreement, and such entry may be made without any legal process whatever, and in any action, suit, or proceeding arising thereout the Landlords may plead, in answer or justification of any alleged trespass or trespasses, the leave and licence of the said Tenant, and this agreement shall be deemed and taken as conclusive evidence thereof.

Arbitration. 29.—ALL QUESTIONS and matters in dispute, and all compensation and allowances upon which the Landlord and Tenant fail to agree, arising under this agreement or in respect of the tenancy hereby created, shall be referred to arbitration in accordance with the provisions of the Agricultural Holdings Act, 1906, but without prejudice to the option of the Landlord in respect of any claim against the Tenant, instead of submitting the same to arbitration, to have recourse to any right of action or other remedy.

Witness to the Signature of Sir David Yule
A. Swift
Villa Esterel Vorranas, Cannes, S. France
Ladys Maid

D. Yule

Author's note: The above is the beginning of the first page and the end of the last page of the tennancy agreement between Sir David Yule and L. A. P. Taylor. It's interesting to note that the witness describes herself as "Lady's Maid"

95

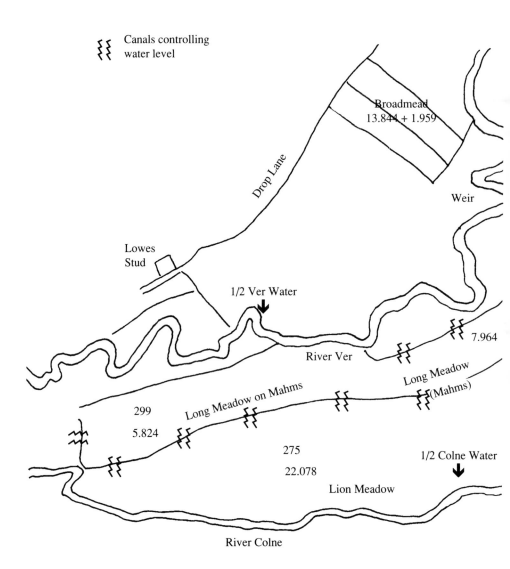

Canals controlling
water level

Broadmead
13.844 + 1.959

Drop Lane

Weir

Lowes
Stud

1/2 Ver Water

7.964

River Ver

Long Meadow
(Mahms)

299

Long Meadow on Mahms

5.824

275

1/2 Colne Water

22.078

Lion Meadow

River Colne

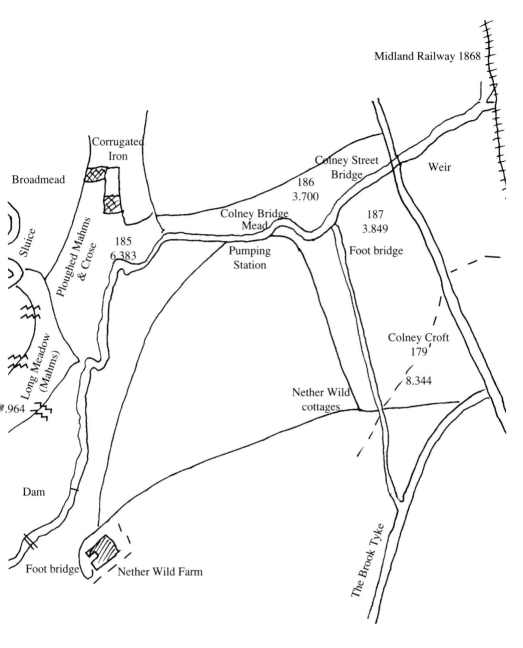

Midland Railway 1868

Corrugated
Iron

Broadmead

Colney Street
Bridge

Weir

186
3.700

Sluice

Colney Bridge
Mead

Ploughed Mahms
& Crose

185
6.383

187
3.849

Pumping
Station

Foot bridge

Colney Croft
179

8.344

Long Meadow
(Mahms)

.964

Nether Wild
cottages

Dam

The Brook Tyke

Foot bridge

Nether Wild Farm

CHAPTER 12

THE SETTLED LAND ACTS 1882 - 1890

After the Dissolution of the monasteries, the real owners of land and property in this area, as in most other parts of the country, were often hidden behind numerous leases at a bank or concealed in the coffers of a family solicitor, only seeing the light of day when one of the family died or a sale of property was being planned.

Two well-known families in this district, the Gapes and the Thellussons, managed to acquire a great deal of the monastery land. The Gape Family Henry Gape was the first recorded member of the Gape family. He was an official at the monastery during the latter part of its working life. After partition, Henry was awarded the Manor of St. Michael. He already owned two large houses situated just north of Romeland. Some years later he was elected Mayor of St. Albans. During his term of office serious rebellion took place led by the town Protestants. The religious impositions of the Catholic Queen Mary were having repercussions of a similar nature all over the country at that time. After one of the principal leaders, George Tankerfield, had been arrested, Queen Mary sent him to St. Albans under armed escort to be burnt at the stake as a warning to the town's Protestants. At that time (August 26th, 1555) Romeland was composed of two sections, Hydes Close and Roumelonde, with a pathway between them. A bonfire and stake were set up near the pathway. Henry Gape's job, as mayor, was to give the order for the bonfire to be lit.

From then onwards, until well into the 20th century, members of the Gape family held official, civil or military duties connected with the town or county, as well as being important proprietors in the district.

Another member of the family, John Gape, is buried beneath a grey stone slab only a step away from the tomb of St. Alban.

His stone bears this inscription:

> *Here lies interred within this vault the body of John*
> *Gape Esq. one of His Majesty's Justice of the Peace for*
> *this County, likewise for the Borough of St. Albans, being*
> *also an Alderman and thrice Mayor of the said Borough*
> *of St. Albans in the reign of King Charles the Second and*
> *Member of Parliament for the same. He departed this*
> *life 20th April 1703 at the age of 80 years.*
> *Ann Gape, his wife, who died on 31st December, 1682,*
> *was also interred here.*

On 23rd June, 1920, a sale by auction of the Gape settled estates took place. They were split into thirty-two different lots and sold separately.

Lot 13 spanned the River Colne at Colney Heath.

Lots 1-8 lay north and south of the road from St. Albans to Hatfield.

Lots 9-12 lay south of the Hatfield railway branch line bordering Baron Rendlesham's land and that of T. Pugh.

Lots 14-15 lay north of the railway line near Roe Green.

Lots 16-18 were lands of the Roehyde and Downs farms in the Parish of North Mimms.

Lot 19 was east of Colney Heath Road between Hutwood and Firwood.

Lot 20 was the wood between lots 5 and 6.

Lot 21 was the land north and south of Sandpit Lane; from Lord Spencer's land to the west, to the border of Nash Hyde Estate.

Lot 22 was land encompassed by that of J. Lloyd and Lord Salisbury to the north and south, and Nash Hyde Estate to the west.

All these lands lay in the parishes of St. Peters Rural, Bishop's Hatfield or North Mimms.

Lots 24 to 30 were in St. Michaels Urban and Rural.

Lot 31 was in St. Michaels Urban (plan included).

Lot 32 comprised the impropriate tithe rent charge arising out of Lots 4,

9 to 13, and 19, plus the Great Northern Railway (commuted value £10. 0. 9).

On October 20th, in the same year that the major sale had taken place, the title to lot 23, which was a part of the Moormill lands, was conveyed from Captain W.N.E.Gape to L.A.P. Taylor, Tom Gee's son-in-law, by the solicitors, Hodding and Clark of Chequer Street, St. Albans, for the sum of £2,250.

Copies of the Conditions of Tom Gee's tenancy sale and his son-in-law's freehold sale, plus the appropriate large scale maps, may be found at the end of this chapter .

The Thellusson Family

Cussan's History of Hertfordshire mentions that one of the Thellusson family, George Woodford, rebuilt the mansion house at Wall Hall near Aldenham, early in the 17th century and renamed it Aldenham Abbey. The mansion, with its beautiful gardens, woods and grounds, has been put to many uses since then. During the Great War it was owned by an American named J. Pierpoint Morgan, who converted part of it into a military hospital. Later on it became a college with an open-air theatre. After being used as a teaching centre for a great number of years, it is now an extension to the University of Hertfordshire. Members of the Thellusson family have been proprietors in this district for many generations under the titles, Lord Rendlesham or Baron Rendlesham.

In pursuance of the School Act of 1841, a day school was proposed for children at the village of Colney Street. The fifth Baron Rendlesham offered a piece of land for one to be erected in the centre of the village alongside the Watling Street in September 1879. A lease of 1 rood 4 perches was accepted by the vicar of Holy Trinity Church, the Revd. Mr. Lipscombe, for a period of 99 years at an annual rent of five shillings, and witnessed by two parishioners, Ilted Nichol and Tom Wright.

100

In 1952 the Parochial Church Council of Frogmore, acting with St. Albans Diocesan Board, purchased the freehold of the school land from the seventh Baron Rendlesham, Percy Edward Thellusson, through an agent, Russell Asquith Woodin, of 22, College Hill, for the sum of £25. The school closed in 1968 and the land and property (excluding the cottage) was sold in 1971 for the sum of £9,250. A condition was made at the time of sale which restricted its use to religious, educational or charitable purposes.

On 13th October, 1908, an agreement was made between the Right Honourable Frederick William Brook Thellusson and Thomas Gee for tenancy of some Moormill lands, listed at the end of chapter 2 and mapped below.

One of the lists, entitled, Colney Street Farm shows the distribution of rents between the Tithe and Lomax family. [Readers of *The Book of Park Street and Frogmore* may recall that it was on Lomax land that the famous golden torc was discovered in 1744.]

A summary of the Agreement was made on October 13th of the same year, giving the total acreage (152 acres, 8 perches) and yearly rent £160. There is also a cost sheet for some bricks used on the Moormill site, and an interesting recipe for horse medicine.

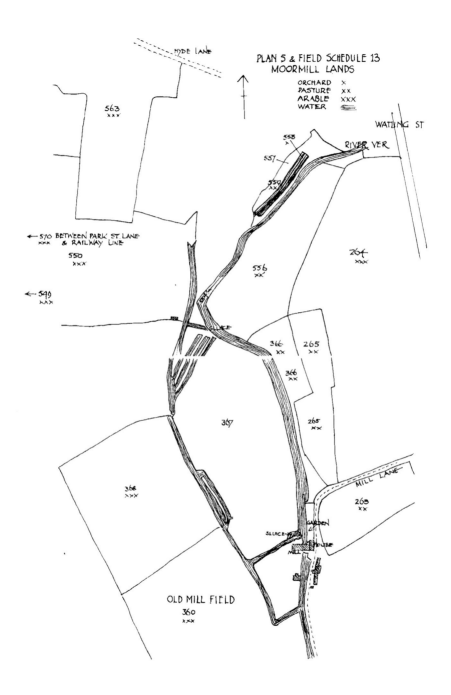

HYDE LANE

PLAN 5 & FIELD SCHEDULE 13
MOORMILL LANDS

ORCHARD   X
PASTURE   XX
ARABLE   XXX
WATER

WATLING ST

563
XXX

558
X
557

RIVER VER

559
XX

264
XXX

←570 BETWEEN PARK ST. LANE
XXX   & RAILWAY LINE

550
XXX

556
XX

←590
XXX

SLUICE

366   265
XX   XX

366
XX

367

265
XX

MILL LANE

368
XXX

263
XX

GARDEN
SLUICE-X
HOUSE
MILL

OLD MILL FIELD
360
XXX

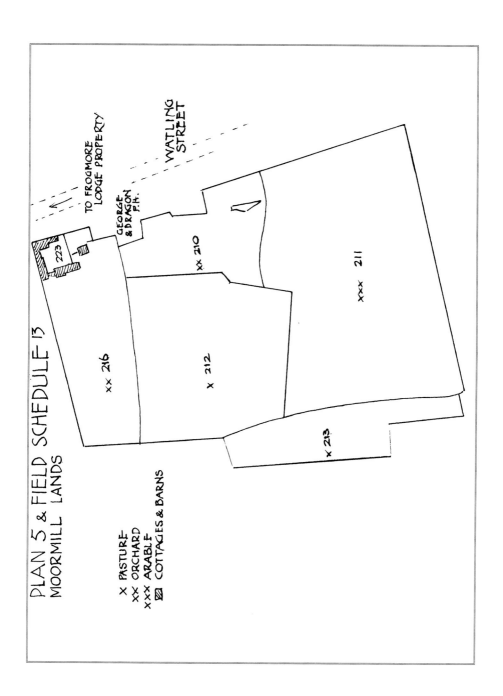

PLAN 5 & FIELD SCHEDULE 13
MOORMILL LANDS

x PASTURE
xx ORCHARD
xxx ARABLE
▨ COTTAGES & BARNS

TO FROGMORE
LODGE PROPERTY

WATLING
STREET

GEORGE
& DRAGON
P.H.

223

xx 216

x 212

xx 210

xxx 211

x 213

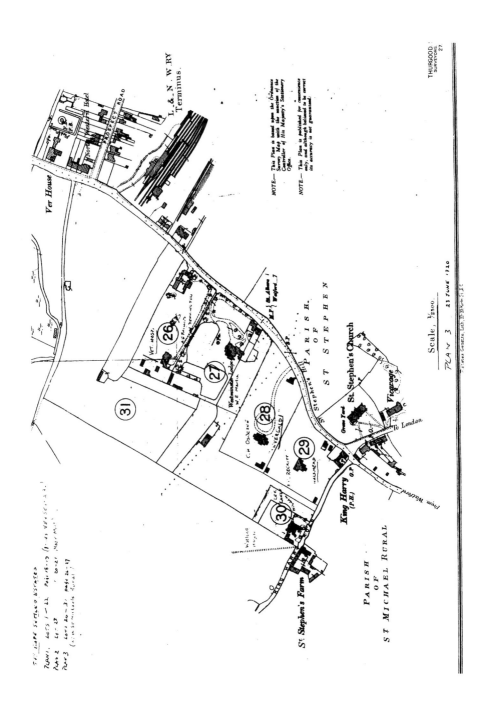

THE HOPE SELFORD ESTATES

PLAN 1. Lots 1 – 21   Page 16–17 (Lots Verses 1, 2.)
PLAN 2. Lot 23   , 20–21 Most Mill
PLAN 3. Lots 24 – 31   page 26 – 27
       (Main St Michaels Rural.)

Vet House

L & N W RY.
Terminus.

PROSPECT ROAD

North Western Hotel

PARISH OF ST STEPHEN

St Stephen's Hill

St Stephen's Church

Vicarage

Green Trees

To London

King Harry
(P.H.)

St Stephen's Farm

PARISH
OF
ST MICHAEL RURAL

From Watford

31

26

27

28

29

30

Scale, 1/2500.

PLAN 3   23 JUNE 1910

NOTE.— This Plan is based upon the Ordnance
Survey Map with the sanction of the
Controller of His Majesty's Stationery
Office.

NOTE.— This Plan is published for convenience
only, and although believed to be correct
its accuracy is not guaranteed.

THURGOOD
SURVEYORS
27

LOT 23

(Coloured *Red* on Plan No. 2) (*large scale*)

A Small Farm and Water Power Corn Mill

KNOWN AS

" Moor Mill "

situate on the River Ver near the Village of Colney Street, lying just off the London Road, about 2½ miles South of St. Albans, three-quarters of a mile from Park Street and Bricket Wood Railway Stations on the London and North Western Railway (St. Albans Branch), and about 1½ miles from Radlett Station on the Midland Railway Main Line, and containing an Area of about

34a.　　0r.　　9p.

of which 19 acres are Grass and 11 acres are Arable, with Good Watercress Beds of about an acre.

Let to Mr. J. Gee on a Yearly Michaelmas Tenancy at the very Moderate Rent of

Per　　£140　　Ann.

THE COMFORTABLE AND WELL-BUILT HOUSE (Brick-built, partly Lath and Plaster and Tile-roofed) contains : Entrance Hall, Drawing Room, Dining Room, Kitchen, Back Kitchen, Larder and Store Room. On the First Floor are 4 Bed Rooms, Lavatory and W.C., and 1 Attic on the Top Floor.

THE BUILDINGS comprise : Cow Shed for 7, Cow Shed for 11, Double Cow Shed for 16 (erected by the Tenant), Milk Cooling Shed, Barn (divided into Mixing House and Loose Box), Range of Open Sheds, 3-stall Stable, 4-stall Stable having Loft over, Range of 3 Piggeries, and Barn.

The Buildings are ample to permit of a Purchaser using them in connection with a further Area of land.

THE WATER-POWER CORN MILL and Buildings comprise : 2 powerful Breast Wheels, driven by the River Ver, with main driving gears and shafting. On the Upper Floor are the Hoppers and Sack-hoisting gear. On the Main Floor are 3 pairs of French and 2 pairs of Grey Stones (one of the latter disused) ; also Smut and Flour-dressing Machines. There are also a Drying Kiln and Van Shed.

Considerable Storage Floor Space exists on the Main and Upper Floors.

Attention is drawn to the AMPLE WATER POWER which, in these days of high-priced coal, is of special and increasing value.

SCHEDULE.

NO. ON PLAN.	DESCRIPTION.	ORDNANCE AREA.	NO. ON PLAN.	DESCRIPTION.	ORDNANCE AREA.
266	Buildings and Grass ..	1.613	Pt. 366	Grass	.565
302	Grass	1.959	367	Do...	12.235
361	Do...	1.617	551	Arable	10.992
Pt. 362	River	1.320	552	Grass	1.485
364	House, Mills, etc. ..	.514	Pt. 553	Watercress Bed	.947
Pt. 365	Watercress Beds ..	.253	Pt. 554	River	.558
				Total Acres ..	34.058

	£	s.	d.
Tithe Commutation—Vicarial	7	14	6
Impropriate	10	0	0
Land Tax	5	16	0

PARTICULARS.

THE VALUABLE ESTATE,

KNOWN AS

MOOR MILL,

SITUATE ON THE RIVER VER,

NEAR COLNEY STREET,

IN THE PARISH OF SAINT STEPHEN,

On the Edgware Road, within 1¼ miles of the Stations on the Midland
and North-Western Railways,

BETWEEN RADLETT & ST. ALBANS,

COMPRISING THE CAPITAL

WATER CORN MILL,

SUBSTANTIALLY BRICK AND TIMBER BUILT,

With Iron Breast Water Wheel (nearly new), and 5 pairs of Stones, Hoppers, Binns, Flour Machines,
Grist Machine, Boulter, Smutter, Chaff Cutter, and the necessary Going Gear, in complete working
order, and good Drying Kiln,

ALSO THE BRICK - BUILT

DWELLING HOUSE,

CONTAINING

5 Bedrooms, 2 Sitting Rooms, Kitchen, Scullery, Brewhouse, Cellar, and good Garden,

CONVENIENT

FARM BUILDINGS AND YARDS,

Comprising 2 Barns, Cart Shed, Cow House, Chaise House, Piggeries, and Stabling for 8 horses;

Index of Principal Characters

Abbots of St Albans

Boreman		11
Geoffrey de Gorham		4
Leofstan		4
Moote, John		7,24
Paul de Caen		3
Richard de Wallingford		
	music	8
	clock	69
	bellows	68
	prayer	6
Robert de Gorham		4

Alding	12
Allen, John	18,19
Anderson	67,69
Anthony	69
Ashby	72
Austin, Mary	91
Babbs, Thomas	11
Bacon, Nicholas	81
Beaument family	13,14,48,49,50
Bigge	90
Bisney	69
Bliss	89
Boff	70,77
Bonwich	75
Bradshaw	69
Bradshaw	69
Bragg, Ronald	28,77
Brock de	80
Brunton	72
Burston	80
Chapman, Earnest & Stan	18-21
Charleton de	80
Christmas	17
Clark	70
Cleaver	74-75
Cokyne	82
Colney Street Farm	30
Cook	72
Cooper	69
Costin	69,73

Dagnall	11
Dayton	70
Denny	81
Dickenson	70,74
Dove	76
Drennon	38,69
Duncan	70
Eames	72
Eason	70
Eccard (smith)	2
Eewer	72,74
Eldred	73
Elwes	73
Elwood	70
Essex - The Earl of	71,83
Evans	74
Ewell	75
Eywood Estate	2,4
Fen	70-71
Ferguson	74
Ffrancys	7
Ffraunceys (blacksmith)	7
Fisk (draper)	92
Fitzhame	80
Fortesque	93
Foster	90
Franklyn	11
Frogmore House - front	79
Fry (Baron of Exchequer)	81
Gape family	98,99,100
Garrett	72
Gee family	26,27,28,30,31,33
George	69,73
Gibbs	82
Giddins family	14,15,16,48,49,50
Goddard, Thomas	12,13
Golape	80
Goodman	77
Gurney	72,74
Hall	90
Hanstead Estate - Sir David Yule	94-97
Hanstead Manor	22
Harding	72

Harris	69
Harrison, Townson	87
Hart	38
Hertfordshire Union	11
Hibbert	71
Honour	76
Hopkinson family	17,18
Hornett	75
Howlett family	27
Hucks	81,82
Humbles	72

Index of Illustrations and Key Events   page

Zeplin raids at Park Street. The Zeplin raid shelter, once a cellar beneath the
mill house office, now lies somewhere under the middle of the main road.   15

Photograph of Park Street looking south. Taken just after the last war, it shows
two parts of the mill house projecting into the main road. Just beyond the car one
gets a glimpse of the two ancient cottages which, together with both sections of
the mill house, had to be demolished to widen the road in circa 1959   42

Hertfordshire Union Chapel (cart shed in the mill yard) see also appendix   11

View of the old mill at Park Street and its modern replacement together with
the owners, Earnest and Stan Chapman.   19/20

Brimley Villas   15

Some of the Howlett family that lived in Park Street's old cottages.   27

Characters in the view south of Park Street. Mrs French and her son Tom are
standing at the corner of Burydell Lane. Behind the small child standing near
them is Fred Isles and his sister Gladys. The four other locals seen in the street
are named Hornett, Littlechild, Sharp and Sweby. Fred was the son of Charlie
Isles, a London architect, who came to Park Street to design and help build the
asylum at Napsbury. He later became Clark of Works and lived at Brimley
Villas. Fred was the original owner of this photograph which he had sent to
his grandmother in London.   40

Park Biri manor house. Forty yards north of this ancient site - now an old
farmhouse in ruins - an archeological dig recently uncovered a "sacrificial boat"
reputed to be around 6,000 years old.   24

A programme of a lively concert held at the Old School in 1912. "Locals entertaining locals."   16

Family tree of the Woodwards at Moor Mill   32

Moor Mill owner and tenant list AD800 - 1989   32

Cost sheets etc. concerning the sale of Moor Mill properties 1875 and 1989   33/37 and 101/106

Agreement between Baron Rendlesham (Thelluson) and Tom Gee concerning Colney Street farm, 13 October 1908.   30/31

Court case between blacksmith and mill owner   49/50

The sad loss of a valuable antique and the conversion of Park Street mill into a factory   51

How the last forge, belonging to 300 years of village blacksmiths, became a bungalow.   52

The sketch of the museum where a forge belonging to George Martin ended up. Also a plan of the district he moved to from Park Street.   54/54

The epilogue of Frank Reed, master blacksmith.   56

Details of rent, paid in kind, to the Abbot of St Albans for property in Radlett.   58
      Plan of early Radlett   64
      Improvements to the roads   59/60
      A glut of benefactors for Radlett   61-63
      A touch of the navy in Radlett   60
      Radlett's halcyon days, 70 years ago   65

Origins of the first squire of Park Street   65

The property of small proprietors in the village:
Anderson family (builders, stonemasons and carpenters)   67
Skeale, Robert (bricklayer)   66
Martin, Will (blacksmith & common brewers)   68

Agreement between Sir David Yule and Leonard Taylor in 1921   94/95
      plan of the land concerned in the agreement   96/97

History of the Noke property   91-93

A brief summary of the history of Holt farm   94/94

Disposal of the last of the Burston property   89

The beginning of How Wood as a village   88/89

The break up of practically the whole of the ancient Burston Estate
12 April 1923   86
     Disposition of Burston in land and lots   82/89

Major-General Biggs - the 18 year old who fought in the Crimean War   90

Mary Austin and Fisk, the draper, who owned the property that became the
Noke Thistle Hotel   91-93

111

3rd July 1869

A New Chapel at Park Street

The old chapel on the waterside at the back of the old mill which has been rented and supplied by the Hertfordshire Union for upwards of sixty years is about to be superceded by a more commodious new one to be erected on an eligible freehold site near the centre of the village*, according to plans and specifications kindly and gratuitously furnished by Mr. Joseph Bennet of St Albans.

At a meeting of the building committee held on Monday last the Rev. T. Watts in the chair, two tenders for the erection and fitting were received; one from Messrs Anderson and Bottom of park Street (jointly) at £210, the other from Mr. Joseph Biggs of St Albans at £211.16.0. The former was accepted. The building is to be commenced forthwith and finished before 15th September.

The chapel will be in the Gothic style, with a flint front and will have open seats for about 120 persons, all free, and will present a very neat appearance.

*Branch Road was being developed around this period.

17th July 1869

Park Street Chapel Dedication Service

A service was held on the occasion of laying the corner stone of the new chapel by Mrs. Inwood of Park Street. During the service it was mentioned that the previous building had been in use for over sixty years, when there was no other place of worship or Sunday School in the village.

25th September 1869

The building being finished, the opening service will take place during the ensuing week. On Wednesday sermons will be preached at 3.00 pm and 6.60 pm by the Rev. W. G. Lewis of Westbourne Grove chapel, London.

The following Sunday, 3rd October there will be sermons at 3.00 pm by the Rev. F. B. Meyer of Regents park College and one at 6.30 pm by the Rev. T. Watts of St Albans.
note:
It is very desirable that the place of worship be entirely free from debt; we believe such an amount is still required to accomplish this as will need liberal collections on these occasions.